It's Funny Because It's TRUE

A Humorous Look at Everyday Occurrences

RONNIE MUNDIS

Copyright © 2019 by Ronnie Mundis

ISBN: 9781700730527

All rights reserved. This book or any portion thereof may not be reproduced or used in any manner whatsoever without the express written permission of the publisher except for the use of brief quotations in a book review.

The Happy Self-Publisher
publish.smile.repeat

www.happyselfpublisher.com

This book is dedicated to my Mother-in-Law, Stella Mundis. She always laughed with me and encouraged me to keep writing.

Table of Contents

Introduction 7
PART ONE: The Early Years 9
Managed Care 11
The Maytag Blues 17
The Leased Phone 21
The Real Estate Dilemma 27
Surviving in the 1990s 33
The Friday Night Date 39
The Gray Hair 45
The Flight 51
The Computer 57
PART TWO: Into the Thick of Things 65
Puddlemania 67
Fifty Something 73
The Bridal Shower 79
A Visit to the New House 85
Pathmark Shoppers 89
The Gold Watch 93
Minding My Own Business 97
The Family Pet 101

PART THREE: Poetic Pause	109
Stella's Poetry Corner: Verses by my Mother-in-Law, *Stella Mundis*	111
PART FOUR: Later On	119
The Noodle Gobbler	121
Corporate America	127
The Eviction	135
Throwback Holiday	143
The Secret	151
PART FIVE: The Fitting End	159
The Good Old Days	161
Boomers Christmas Dinner	169
Online Dating	173
S T O P	177
Boot Scooting	185
And on We Go!	191
Acknowledgments	193
About the Author	195

Introduction

In the 1950s, new inventions were coming into American households at a rapid pace – at least one every five years (this was considered rapid back then). It started with the small black and white television, followed by the coveted extension telephone. All households had one phone that was placed in the living room or on the kitchen wall, but a second phone was a real luxury. These plastic machines had to be installed by a telephone company technician and cost the customer a monthly rental fee plus an installation fee which was paid to the one and only telephone company. Polaroid Cameras (cameras that developed your pictures instantly), colored televisions and microwaves popped up in the mid-to-late 1960s. Bank credit cards became popular and accessible in the 1980s, and computers became a fixture in American homes in the 1990s. Scientists developed a system of connecting America to the internet by using the telephone lines which were connected from the phone outlet through the wires to a special box at the telephone pole. Thus, you would hear a dial tone when trying to access the internet. Those of us in the Baby Boomer generation clearly remember these developments in technology. However, for the benefit of younger folks who may read this book, I wanted to describe the hard times of slow technology. Some of my stories reflect those difficulties. In looking back, I realize that those times were a necessary step to achieving the technology we all enjoy today. The ability to laugh at technical difficulties and a variety of life's situations through good times and bad is always needed. These stories are my attempts to see the humor in everyday occurrences.

PART ONE:

Early Days

1

Managed Care

Sniffle, sniffle, achoo! Sniffle, sniffle, achoo! Those distinct sounds of illness coming from down the hall were a signal that there is a sick person in my house. I hope whoever it is does not want to see a doctor because I am not, I repeat **not**, going to make an appointment with our managed care facility.

Two months ago, a pair of swollen eyes and a stuffy nose woke me from a deep sleep indicating that I had come down with my yearly sinus infection. Relief involves calling for an appointment, going into a sanitized medical office, having a specialist look down my throat, and leaving with a prescription in hand. Always a sure remedy until 12 months later when similar symptoms develop. This has been happening once a year for the past five years, so I know exactly what is wrong and what will cure me.

Unfortunately, handling this situation requires that I see my HMO care physician, and arranging that demands some fancy talking. In today's managed care society, one cannot merely call and obtain an appointment with one's regular physician without answering a series of intimidating questions. That would be way too easy.

Today I was connected to a young apprentice who was determined to prevent me from reaching my goal of seeing a doctor. The conversation went like this:

"Why do you think you are sick, Ma'am?"

I described my symptoms: swollen eyes, stuffy nose, sore throat, and cotton head. Then the dreaded question was presented, "Do you have any mucus discharge, Ma'am?"

Even though common sense dictates that a stuffy nose does not have a discharge, I play the managed care insurance game and respond, "Why yes I do."

It's Funny Because It's True

"What color is your mucus, Ma'am?"

The appropriate reply of "green" was given.

Content I had answered all the directives correctly, I was surprised when instead of receiving an appointment, another question was solicited. "What shade of green is your mucus, Ma'am?"

My blood shot eyes stared at the phone in disbelief and before I could reconsider my response, I blurted out, "What the hell kind of question is that? This is ridiculous! Look, I know my body and I know what is wrong with me. I am not a frequent caller. I am a once a year, one type of affliction kind of gal and I am currently suffering with my annual sinus infection. You know what, if you are too busy, I do not even need an appointment. Just have any doctor call in a prescription for an antibiotic and I won't bother you people anymore."

An eerie silence prevailed as I imagined my suggestion was being considered. That theory was thwarted when a more mature voice came on the line and declared, "Doctor studied at the university for six long years, so he could learn to diagnose illnesses. What expertise do you have, Ma'am? If you are that well-informed, feel free to cure yourself and please do not partake of our services."

Realizing the remedy for my condition was rapidly slipping away, I swallowed my pride and replied, "Wait, would you please repeat the question?"

"Well now," smirked Gal Friday, "that's more like it." She enunciated slowly, "What shade of green is your mucus, Ma'am?"

To this I answered, "Hunter green, a dark hunter green."

Satisfied, as hunter green was listed as a shade requiring immediate attention, I was advised to come right over, and she would fit me in with someone on staff.

Who says aggressive behavior does not work? I had asserted myself and I was going to be seen by an able-bodied health provider, and I was going to be seen *today*!

It's Funny Because It's True

I arrived at the office and sashayed my way to the front desk. I gave my name and announced I was here to see A Doctor.

Looking down the list the receptionist exclaimed, "Ah yes, I see your name now. It is right here under Little Miss Self Diagnosis. Unfortunately, A Doctor does not have time to see You, however, Nurse Practitioner will be happy to see YOU."

"Listen sweetie, anybody I see will be fine, perfectly fine," I stated, while pointing a finger in her face. "In fact, my condition is so obvious even you can look down my throat, diagnose a sinus infection, and give me my meds."

After being escorted to a room and instructed to take off all my clothes for an exam that should only require looking down my throat, I realized that my sarcastic comments may have had a few consequences. My suspicions were validated when Nurse Ratched arrived and began administering a battery of tests which would make any medic in the armed services proud. I was ready to stand at attention and salute, when she instructed me to swing my head down to my knees.

Shocked, I repeated, "You want me to swing the thing sitting on my shoulders that feels like a 30-pound weight to my knees and expect me to stand up again?" Her surprised look prompted this request, "If I can perform that impossible feat will you look down my throat and please give me some medicine?"

"Why yes I will, because this happens to be the last part of your exam," she jeered.

Somehow, I managed to swing my head to my knees, return to an upright position and triumphantly gave her a wobbly smile. As I sat there holding my head, my ears began to ring, my eyes began to throb, and remarkably. my nose did start to drain a little.

Totally disoriented, a series of incoherent moans streamed out when I was asked, "Now how do you feel?" Those moans must have been the correct answers because shortly afterwards, I was headed home with a prescription in hand.

This memorable visit to my local managed care facility was still fresh in my mind when my daughter emerged from her room coughing, sneezing, and mumbling that she needed to see a doctor. Instead of offering to make an appointment for her, she was shocked when I handed her the phone, the phone number, the answers to the required questions, patted her on the back and said, "Here you go and good luck with that."

2

The Maytag Blues

"Mom, we have a big problem here," was another remark coming from my daughter, who had something negative to say about absolutely everything in our house since she graduated from college and moved home. The choice to ignore her changed when water starting gushing from the laundry room along with a loud boom as Big Bertha, my sturdy 10-year-old Maytag washer, spun her last, and with a mighty roar, gave up the fight. The gauntlet had been thrown. I had enough of the patch-together remedies, and in no uncertain terms laid into my handyman husband. "This is no longer fixable! I want a new washing machine TODAY!! Might as well buy a new dryer to replace that 10-year-old monstrosity in the corner too!" I don't know if it was the tone of my voice or the fact that my mother was coming for a visit, but instead of an argument, he mumbled "okay," and we were off to the local discount appliance warehouse.

Upon approaching the store and realizing the opportunity to purchase new wash day conveniences only comes around once in 10 years, I wanted one with all the bells and whistles. If one was available that folds the clothes and walks them to the closet, regardless of price, I wanted it! Of course, my bargain-conscious other half hunted down an oversized sturdy white object with barely two cycles to its name. The price was right, but it was so outdated that it was one step away from the old washboard by the creek. However, since we were buying not one but two appliances (even though the dryer was still functioning), I opted to take what I could get. After haggling over the price, our purchase was made, and we drove our truck in line to the dock so the loading crew could strut their stuff.

That day it was 98 degrees in the shade, and we were in ol' blue (our trusty old blue pickup), who recognizes no seasons as the heat and air conditioner control provide the same results (lots and lots of hot air). Unable to stay in the cab, we entertained ourselves by standing outside and watching Manuel and the boys load the truck in front of us. After 30 minutes of watching this team bundle and wrap and bundle and wrap, I observed their system closely so I could figure out what was taking so long. The members of that gang were working hard at loading two appliances on the vehicle in front of us in the following way: they wrapped each one in heavy plastic, covered them with a foam blanket to prevent dents, and then these appliances were enclosed in cardboard and labeled. Satisfied the goods were well protected, the merchandise was then anchored to the truck with a heavy rope. Coincidently these folks were getting a washer and dryer just like the ones we just purchased (small world). With their purchases secured, those happy shoppers flashed us big smiles and waved as they departed the parking lot. Finally, it was our turn, so I eagerly gave my sales slip to the hardworking stock man and waited anxiously as he took his dolly into the store to extract my coveted washing instruments. Five minutes later he returned with an empty dolly, spoke rapidly in Spanish to his two cohorts, and they all exited into a small room to my right. We thought they were taking a break until after another 15 minutes with no workers in sight, we came to realize that they were just not coming back. Immediately a supervisor was summoned. After an intense argument between the supervisor and his crew, none of which we understood, it was discovered that our new washer and dryer were not coming home with us but, in fact, were on their way to Maryland. I don't know what the people in front of us bought, but they left with my dryer and my two-cycle washer and I wanted them back! I wanted them back NOW!! That couple probably bought a $75 table and left with $700 of my merchandise.

A fortunate outcome of this mistake was that we took home a washer that may not have had all the bells and whistles, but had at least a few more bells for the same price as that white elephant. They heard me exclaim as we drove out of sight, "Only in America folks, and to all a good night."

3

The Leased Phone

"Congratulations! You have just pole vaulted into the 1980's!" This sarcasm came from one of my cynical daycare parents after I proudly displayed ownership of my first phone. Remember when everyone had to lease their telephones? The sales pitch included wire maintenance protection for all phone wires along with the luxury of a replacement phone for the mere price of $12 every three months. So, as the years went by, even though the price rose from $12 to $21, I kept paying this fee. Therefore, when the old kitchen phone refused to ring anymore, I looked forward to finally receiving something for my money. Five years ago, in a similar situation, I was directed to a modern distribution center and chose a lovely replacement from several models and colors. Today, upon inquiry, the directions given were to drive down a back alley to a dilapidated shoe repair shop to make my selection. After requesting a new working communication device, the store owner suggested I stop all this foolishness and just go to a Kmart to purchase a new phone. However, since I had been paying my $21 fee every three months over the last 10 years, I insisted on receiving something for my money. Our lively discussion ended when the shoe repair man shook his head, mumbled, "Okay, okay." He grabbed my broken powder blue wall phone and disappeared into the back room to see if he could find something compatible. After 15 minutes, he emerged and shoved a strange looking turquoise object at me. When I asked if this was actually a telephone and if he had something more presentable, he replied, "Lady there are only two styles available. It is this or black. Take your choice." I snatched that funny looking thing from his hands, thanked him for his wonderful advice, and raced home to plug in this miracle of miracles.

It's Funny Because It's True

As soon as Alexander Graham Bell's greatest invention was unwrapped and displayed on the kitchen table I heard, "What the hell is that thing?" My 15-year-old, who does not believe in sugarcoating anything, had expressed herself. She followed with, "It is the ugliest thing I have ever seen, and don't you even think about hanging that on our wall."

Soon the suggestion to purchase a new phone with a built-in answering machine was bantered about. However, certain that as soon as I stopped paying the monthly fee for my wire maintenance, my wires would fray, I resisted and decided to get another opinion. My investigation included calling my mother for advice. Confident that if I am still paying this charge, surely my 70-year-old mother was doing the same.

Imagine my surprise when she loudly answered, "I cannot believe you are still paying that wire maintenance fee. Of course, I bought my own phone years ago."

Feeling embarrassed that I stupidly spent a tidy sum of money to lease a phone when I could have bought one for a fraction of the cost, that turquoise thing was quickly thrown in a bag, and driven back to the store where the necessary papers were signed to end my lease contract. I attempted to justify my behavior by explaining, "Of course I only paid for this coverage so I could get the wire maintenance protection." That excuse was rejected when the shoemaker's (a/k/a the AT&T rep) head jerked up as he peered over his bifocals and asked, "What's that you say, wire maintenance what?"

After questioning that he, being a representative of the phone company, should be more knowledgeable about his product, he replied, "Lady, I bought my phone ten years ago for $15 and I never heard of any wire maintenance." Feeling like a fool for paying for a service that no longer exists, I slinked home to gather my thoughts and install my new purchase.

An hour later, the Avon Lady was at my door to deliver my order. As our conversation progressed, she informed me that her telephone was not functioning properly, and did I know where the nearest trade-in center was located. Eager to pass on information concerning the

It's Funny Because It's True

AT&T farce, I encouraged her to stop paying for this service and immediately buy her own phone. Confused she replied, "But, If I don't lease, what will I do about my wire maintenance, dear?"

4

The Real Estate Dilemma

Help! The realtors are after me, the realtors are after me! Since 1989, my husband and I have dabbled in the real estate market trying to secure our fortunes. Chasing this goal, we pursued several agents to request they share their hot tips to alert us of a fantastic deal. The other day, our foresight paid off when we received a phone call and wrote down the following directive.

First, go to the worst part of the city. Second, bring a step ladder as there is no front stoop. Third, take a crowbar to pry the wooden barrier off the front door. Fourth, hoist yourself into the house and, with your flashlight in hand, ignore the holes in the walls and roof. Finally, look at the deal of a lifetime. The clincher is, we were told, these beauties haven't hit the market yet, so we have the first stab at them. I am sure some brave soul with a strong constitution and bullet proof vest will make a fortune here. However, since the location was on a street where my better half's truck was bombarded with rocks by the neighborhood coalition last year, we regretfully had to pass on this once-in-a-lifetime opportunity. Yes, we have met many a fine professional in the real estate field and some are so noteworthy, they bear telling about.

One man I refer to affectionately as Zippy the Zipper. Today was the day we were finally going to look at a house with a pool. Never mind that it sat between a Burger King and a Pizza Hut (all the better to entertain my guests with). It had my coveted in-ground pool and we just had to have a look.

Upon arriving at our destination, a large, sloppy looking male realtor greeted us by exiting his car while buttoning his shirt. Obviously, he hadn't finished dressing, as I noticed he had also neglected to zip his fly. I thought it strange that his underwear was flesh colored, but being a married lady, I remained silent and averted my eyes for the entire tour. Then my business partner whispered, "We have flesh, we have flesh." Apparently, this man had neglected to don his underwear. Could this be a new technique in Realtor 101?

Convinced this was the house of my dreams, I was anxious to inspect every nook and cranny. When my questions were answered vaguely, it became apparent that, even though this was Zippy's listing, he knew little about it. When asked where the pool area was located, he replied, "I believe you can see it from the back or maybe from the middle bedroom window." Sure enough if you peered through that window you could see a pool with a barbeque area, but when asked how we could obtain access to it, he was unable to direct us and actually suggested we go to Burger King for our burgers. Needless to say, there would be no SOLD sign posted that day.

Another experience involved the ever-competent Bumble Arty. Following the system we learned from our $180 How to Buy Real Estate with No Money Down Course, we contacted the listing agent of a potential property instead of our regular competent agent. This is where our troubles began.

First, Bumble missed the showing appointment. When I called to inquire where he was, he seemed to be unaware that we had an engagement and suggested we meet the following night, which was a Wednesday. Since this property was a HUD repossession and being somewhat familiar with the process (bids must be submitted on Tuesday after the listing appears in the paper), I questioned Mr. Arty several times concerning the deadline for sending our offer. He assured me that the closing date was next Tuesday and not to worry as he uses Federal Express for all his bids so they will get there in plenty of time. Alrighty then!

We wrote the contract and handed over our good faith money. The next Monday I was not surprised when I received a call from a very apologetic real estate professional. It seems that as Mr. Competent was gathering his contracts together to post in the mail, he was advised that the deadline was not this Tuesday but, in fact, had been the previous Tuesday. A vision of a confident guy in a three-piece suit stopping Arty, as he was licking his envelope, to ask, "Hey Arty (snicker, snicker), what are you doing? That house was sold last week," flashed through my head. I began to laugh for getting exactly what I deserved for following the book instead of my instincts. Arty, sensing a jovial mood, continued to inform us that the winning bid was lower than our bid and had he submitted his paperwork on time, we would have gotten the house. Should anyone in their right mind divulge this information? I mean, haven't licenses been lifted for less serious offenses?

Do not believe that toothless man on TV stating in broken English, "I have no job, no credit, no life, and I buy house with no money and am now a millionaire." Having tried this method, I am sure that as long as Bumble and Zippy are on the job, the millions of dollars to be made in real estate will safely remain in someone else's pocket.

5

Surviving in the 1990s

It seemed to me that every time I made a transaction in the 1990s world, I got an equal but negative reaction. My experience was as follows.

Purchasing a major appliance turned into a nightmare. Either I was charged the wrong price, the charge was on someone else's card, their charge was on my card, or I was given back the wrong charge card. Every time I went out the door, I cringed because I knew an extra trip or a day's worth of phone calls would be needed to clear up another misunderstanding. Luckily, I worked at home and had access to a phone and a fax machine. One practically needed a secretary to survive the finances of the 1990s.

Ronnie Mundis

Do not, I repeat, do not attempt to move and keep your old phone number. Nothing against AT&T, but it cannot be done. I know because I tried, and I failed. After speaking to a courteous telephone operator, who assured me that keeping the same number and my 10-cents-a-minute long distance rate would be no problem, I was thrilled! Thrilled, that is, until I received a $60 bill for three long distance phone calls. It seems instead of the 10 cents a minute plan, I was given the business plan of 40 cents a minute any time of the day or night. That plus several surcharges for having the luxury of a business line, which I did not request or want, accounted for this exorbitant bill. Not to worry, I have access to a phone, and I am sure this can be fixed in a jiffy, right? WRONG!! Even though I followed the correct protocol, I now must spend my day contacting not only the local phone company, but also several business plan 800 numbers to correct this situation. And of course, since each individual phone company can only access their own company's private screen, I am responsible for watching my bills and faxing them each month to three different locations until all the credits come through. I wonder how many bewildered customers just pay the full amount to save themselves a lot of time and trouble.

Enraged, I demanded to know who was responsible for this screw up. The forthcoming answer was, "Why nobody is responsible." Let me rephrase that question. "Who made the error that caused me to have a business phone account?" Again, the answer was: Nobody. The phone company seems to exist in its own world of ignorance where no one is at fault for anything. Oh, wouldn't it be grand if we could all find our way into that wonderful Nirvana?

Determined to get every credit due, I was looking at my bill deciding which company to fax what portion to first when: Ring, ring, Avon calling! It was the Avon Lady complaining that her phone account was changed to a business plan that is charging her 40 cents a minute. When she called to voice her displeasure because she never requested this change, they responded that nobody at their company made a mistake and therefore she must be at fault. Anyway, as one thing led to another, this savvy cosmetic vender questioned the oh so pleasant operator about their leased phone policy. Several transfers later revealed that over the past 20 years she had paid at least $500 to lease her two rotary phones, and returning them to end her lease agreement with The King of Wireless Communications would save her a lot of money. Knowing this process involved struggling to tow those phones to her car, finding a handicapped parking space, and lugging them behind her walker to cancel her contract led to this request: "Hon, could you take pity on a handicapped senior citizen and let me keep my phones and still end my lease?" A glimmer of hope existed as one humane employee suggested that since rotary phones were not in demand anymore and a pretty penny had already been paid for their use maybe, just this once, AT&T could bend the rules. That glimmer of hope was extinguished when Carrie, the Supervisor, I mean Carrie the go-by-the book, I-am-climbing-the-corporate-ladder Supervisor, was approached for permission and replied, "Absolutely not! There will be no exceptions to this rule for any reason because AT&T may need those two rotary phones someday."

It's Funny Because It's True

Upon hearing this tale, I began to bash our Switchboard Susies, Corporate America, and phone company policies when, click – my phone went dead. Now I am not accusing anyone of listening in but as soon as my complaints got hot and heavy, I was suspiciously cut off (complete silence, no dial tone, nothing). A half-hour later, the dial tone came back on and I thought it was business as usual. Business as usual until my son informed me our home phone number that we had for the past 20 years was now assigned to a heavily accented Spanish speaking man. Coincidentally that very day, Ronnie's Daycare had a large, expensive advertisement running in the local newspaper. When dialing for a haven for their lads and lassies instead of hearing, "You have reached Ronnie's Daycare, hugs and kisses, we love children," those mamas were treated to a swinging single's message. I bet they dropped their baby bottles and bibs when they heard Carlos Montalban say, "Hello Daahling you are simply Maahvelous. If you want to swing with Hector press one, chill with Enrico, press two." What number do you press if you want to change diapers with Ronnie?

Ronnie Mundis

I am sitting here looking at a very large bill that got absolutely no response. Upon requesting a refund from the Corporate Conveyer of Messages, I was told, "Certainly not, because no one at AT&T made this mistake and lady, you should be grateful that you did not lose your daycare license for having such a disgusting message." That settles it. Tomorrow I am going to retire from the daycare business and help people straighten out their phone bills for a living.

6

The Friday Night Date

"What is that smell?" That was a question I asked one of the young fathers, who came to pick up his child at my daycare on a Friday afternoon.

"What smell?" he asked.

"You know, it is not quite a perfume, but a cross between an air freshener and a candle scent."

"Do you mean my aftershave?" he replied.

"Yeah, aftershave that's it," was my response as I looked at him and noticed he was dressed in clothes other than his usual work garments. "Hey, you look nice," came out before I had a chance to think. "Are you going somewhere?"

Ronnie Mundis

When he answered that he was taking his wife out tonight, I stared at him with a confused look as if he had uttered a foreign phrase. *Out on a Friday night, smelling good with nice clothes on*, I mused. *Hmm…. Now let me think. I have been married for 20 years and my memory is fading, but I am certain I know what that is called.* "I see it now. It is called a date. A Friday Night Date. That's what I want. I want a Date!"

An uncomfortable silence followed my outburst as he gave me a strange look, grabbed his little girl and headed out the door.

That afternoon, when my significant other came home, I was ready for him. Oh boy, was I ready. With a scowl on my face, hands on my hips and my foot just a'tapping away, I demanded "I want a date and I want it tonight!"

"Whoa, just a minute now, I was going to save this as a surprise, but Old Walt asked us to come over this evening because he wants to show us something."

"Well okay then, that's more like it." I'm not sure this warrants a splash of Chanel No 5, as it was not exactly what I had in mind, but I guess you have to start somewhere.

Two hours later we found ourselves in Walt's living room discussing his favorite topic, The Farm. A natural born storyteller, he amused us with interesting facts about surviving on a farm in the 1920s. Being a sucker for the good old days, I was charmed and hung onto his every word. Thrilled to hear stories of his mother sewing red and white seersucker underwear for all of her 17 children and of course, the inevitable 10-foot high snowstorm tale where life, as you know it, ended until all the able-bodied men shoveled the train tracks so the mail could get through. Then Walt began to recite his favorite theme of all: "The castration of hogs."

Last year when we were at a restaurant celebrating his 79th birthday, he went on this tangent. After loudly describing the procedure for the third time in no uncertain terms, I happened to glance to my right, noticed a lady seated there holding her stomach, turning a weird shade of green muttering, "Could you people talk about something else as I am trying to eat a pork chop here?" Quickly, the conversation switched to Walt's second favorite subject: Sex in the 1920s.

In the unrestricted environment of Walt's living room, any topic was fair game, so issues concerning how meat from castrated hogs tastes better than regular hogs and grain fed chicken eggs taste better than wild fed chicken eggs were bantered about. Bored with this conversation and just as the Wheel of Fortune puzzle was about to be solved, Walt shouted, "Come into the kitchen, youngsters, I want to show you something!"

Hot Dog! Here is the highlight of my date. Anticipating the excitement, I rushed into the kitchen and sat at the edge of my chair. Our host slowly sauntered in, picked up an orange, peeled it, and cut it into sections. Then without offering us a bite, ate the whole thing. Thanking him for an enjoyable evening we exited out the front door and sped home,

Much later, the conversation coming from our bedroom sounded like this. "Tonight, we went to an 80-year-old man's house, listened to life as it was lived in the 1920s, then watched him peel and eat an orange."

To that my hubby replied, "I know."

Then at the same time we both said, "The scary thing is, I enjoyed it."

Maybe I should compare, or rather take notes, from my daycare father on Monday to figure out what went wrong.

7

The Gray Hair

"Ronnie, you look really old today." Surprised as this comment was coming from my mother, whose job it is to bolster my self-esteem, I ran to the bathroom to look in my mirror, mirror on the wall. Instead of Snow White, there was the image of an old gray-haired witch looking back at me. Something ought to have been done about this condition yesterday.

Realistically, I know I should have called to make an appointment with a professional hair stylist or at least gone to the local beauty supply house for the proper materials. However, having no time to spare, I cast those thoughts aside and ran to the nearest supermarket to purchase a magic potion that would turn those curly gray locks into something more youthful.

The last time I decided to wash that gray right outta my hair, I found myself leaning away from the lackluster medium brown color towards a more exciting auburn. Just something different to give myself a vibrant, eye-popping splash. Shortly after this dye job, I stepped out of the car to attend my daughter's volleyball game and was greeted with "Mom, get back in That Car." It seems that when the sun's rays hit my coiffure, instead of a tint of exotic auburn, a shade of essence of Bing Cherry ensued. Not to worry, I wanted a splash and a splash I got. So with my purple head held high, I proudly marched into that gymnasium and cheered my team onto victory. That color washed out in six weeks and, I must admit, once I got used to it, I liked it. With age comes knowledge, and I have since been careful to always pick the same dull brown hair dye when the occasion warrants.

Don't ask me why, blame it on my forgetfulness, or maybe I was just feeling risqué that day, because I opted for a darker shade of

It's Funny Because It's True

brown instead of the medium tint. The next day my gray hair disappeared, all right. In its place, I was gifted with a headful of bluish, black locks. So what? I seldom leave the house, and no one sees me but six daycare young'uns who only notice what they are being served for lunch. I'll just continue looking in the mirror once a day and forget it, right? WRONG!!

Two days later as I was serving the little varmints their daily ration of peanut butter and jelly, my observant, soon-to-be-six-year-old comments, "Miss Ronnie do you know you have black hair?' This sets off a chain reaction where every child individually repeats, "Miss Ronnie I like your new black hair."

Gritting my teeth, I answered each one with, "Thank you so much for noticing," until we came back to the main culprit, my precocious soon-to-be-first-grader.

He then continues, "So, is it a wig?"

I reply, "No, it is not a wig."

He counters, "Did you dye your hair?" A hush falls over the kitchen as six pairs of eyes look my way as they anxiously wait for my response.

"Yes, I did Mister Smarty Pants, because I want to look like Snow White, okay?"

No longer able to restrain himself, my husband quips, "She looks more like Elvis, if you ask me."

A rousing burst of laughter rises from the peanut gallery for no apparent reason, as I am sure this group doesn't know Elvis from Little Richard. Then they all settled down as I glared at my significant other who was laughing so hard at his impromptu witticism that he could not compose himself.

That night after receiving expert advice from my teenage daughter, I armed myself with a gallon of warm water and half a dozen lemons to attempt to lighten the mess on top of my head. This process succeeded in rinsing the black color out of only the gray strands. Now the gray is more pronounced as it is sprinkled among the midnight black, changing me from a respectful Elvis to an aging Liberace.

I was prepared to put this whole nasty experience behind me and function as usual until my Avon Lady showed up to deliver my order.

It's Funny Because It's True

She took one look at my gray/ black hair and, as if I planned this effect, commented, "Oh my, that gray/black look is very aging on you, Sweetheart."

8

The Flight

The sun is shining, the birds are singing, and the air feels fresh outside. "Come on kids, Ronnie's Daycare is going to do something unconventional today. We are going for a morning walk!" Six heads whipped around as blurry eyes left the latest Sesame Street episode to glare at me. Undaunted I continued, "Once around the block with vim and vigor, gang! It will get the old blood circulating."

Hesitant because they did not comprehend the words blood and circulating, we got off to a slow start. Nevertheless, soon six pairs of feet were running ahead while I kept pace behind the herd. This day, overwhelmed by the bright sunshine and crisp air, I was pumping my fists, lifting my face to the sky, and hurrying my step to keep up with the little devils. Remember the saying, "Watch where you are going?" I found out there is a reason for that phrase. Even though every nook, cranny and crevice of that sidewalk was familiar, when you are walking with your nose in the air, accidents do happen. One minute I was whistling a merry tune, swinging my arms, maintaining an aerobic heartbeat to make Richard Simmons proud. The next minute my body was launched on a human flight, the length to be challenged in the Guinness Book of World Records.

Soaring up, up and away, numerous thoughts went through my head: 1. Position my body to glide past the weedy lawn and head straight for the persnickety neighbor's yard. You know, the one who fertilizes and reseeds every year to provide a soft, thick cover for my perfect landing; 2. Spread your arms so you can explain that no, Miss Ronnie did not fall down, but yes, Miss Ronnie was trying to fly like a bird; 3. Once this unfortunate incident is over, never ever walk this way again. Accepting the situation on hand, there was no other option but to spread my

It's Funny Because It's True

wings, enjoy the flight, and prepare for my descent.

As my face connected with Mother Earth, skimming two inches of grass off the top and sinking into the muck below, my head stopped when it hit a pair of spit-polished boots that were connected to none other than my finicky neighbor whose lawn I had just violated. Instead of offering a hand up and asking me if I was okay, he screamed, "Go away and take your brats with you!" He did an about face, ran into his house, and slammed the door. Realizing there would be no assistance coming from that Good Samaritan, an adrenaline boost helped me to get on my feet, and hobble to the corner where six energetic little people were chomping at the bit like race horses waiting to come out of the gate.

Our excursion ended when my tiny tots ran into the house to position themselves back in front of the TV while my aching body limped behind. Misjudging the door threshold, I lost my balance and BOOM! went down like a sack of potatoes. You could've heard a pin drop as six small mouths gaped open as for the second time today, they witnessed Miss Ronnie lying on the ground in an unsightly position.

The next day I was in agony. After all, a 49-year-old, out of shape woman cannot survive two major falls in one day without having something go out of whack. Not to worry, I have a chiropractor who will push those bones right back into the correct position. After checking with his answering machine which assured me that yes, the doctor does have office hours on Wednesday evening and yes, if you are a regular patient, you do not need an appointment, I wisely drove off in search of relief. Carefully my body lumbered out of my car and slowly approached the door of my miracle worker. Anticipating a good dose of sympathy accompanied by the ministration of those magical hands, I grasped the doorknob and pulled hard only to realize that it was not going to budge. As I lifted my fist to give a few hard knocks, the glow of the sunset bounced off a yellow stickie note in the window which read: GONE FISHING. BE BACK MONDAY.

Gone fishing in 1998 in the middle of the week while I stand here in extreme pain! Does this man think he is Sheriff Andy of Mayberry or what? The saying, "God helps those who help themselves," suddenly flashed through my mind. Following that advice, I stopped at the nearest liquor store, bought a bottle of wine and headed home.

9

The Computer

Back in the 1990s, it seemed to be a popular consensus that to be a happy, well-adjusted household, you needed a computer in your home. It was strongly suggested that in order to become an integral part of the business world, I would need not only a regular computer, but the Grand Daddy of all machines. So I became the proud owner of an instrument that, in layman's terms, has *fast speed* (don't know where it is running to) and *sound* (Loud, Loud Sound). In fact, when turned on, it sounds like the Philharmonic Orchestra. The selling feature of purchasing this wonder of wonders was that my son promised to spend time at home to install and instruct me on how to operate it. The time he intended to spend was his sick leave for recuperation after minor surgery.

Unfortunately, shortly after my IBM was delivered, the noise of my daycare toddlers caused him to prematurely exit back to his home in the mountains. There I stood with a very large cancelled check in my hand, ignored my husband's I-told-you-so comments, and stared at this modern-day invention that I hadn't a clue how to operate.

What's a person to do? Admit she made a humongous, expensive boo-boo? Certainly not! Spend more money? Yeah that's it. Undaunted I proceeded to not only subscribe to the internet, but also have a private phone line installed for the convenience of anyone who can figure out how to use this thing. Satisfied that all necessary tools had been provided, I sat down and diligently followed the directions of how to access the internet. After two hours of hearing a constant busy signal, help was solicited from my teenage daughter. After spending five minutes at the keyboard, she sarcastically commented, "Mom, something is wrong with your new phone line."

It's Funny Because It's True

"I knew that, ha, ha! Just testing to see if you learned anything in that school of yours."

A quick call to Bell Tell and voila! – the next day a worn-out, middle-aged telephone repair man shuffled through my door to solve the problem. He looked forlorn as he opened his toolbox and silently pursued all avenues of repair. Eight frustrating hours of hard work testing all the wires and installing another phone line with no positive outcome in sight, resulted in summoning the Supervisor of troubleshooters to the location of the malfunctioning line. As soon as this big boss sat down, he discovered the call waiting feature from my old phone number was still active, quickly pushed a button, and, just like that, my computer was connected.

With everything finally in order, I gave the command, "Let the emailing begin." Ready to email until I dropped, I sent computer mail to everyone I had an address for and sat down to wait for their replies.

In the morning, I booted up (that means *turned on*) my computer, went on the internet to check my emails, and was shocked to discover the screen was empty (no letters, no advertisements, nothing). Thinking I may have sent something inappropriate, I called the recipients of my efforts to inquire where the heck their responses were. Surprise, surprise – these people were confused because they were sending emails and not getting answers from me. Reluctantly, I connected my computer into the phone outlet and heard nothing, absolutely no dial tone. Now even though I am paying for two phone lines, a computer bill, an installation bill, and an internet bill, I must place long distance toll calls to find out where my emails went. In a state of much agitation, I summoned AT&T and demanded SERVICE!!

Lo and Behold, on Friday afternoon, a second telephone repair man appeared at my door. Halfheartedly glancing out the window, as I was expecting Old Reliable, my head whipped around when what to my wondering eyes did appear, but a gorgeous hunk without any reindeer! Mama Mia, what is this?!

This guy wore a gleaming white hard hat, shiny sunglasses, form-fitted tee shirt, tight jeans and spit-polished boots. Here I sit, a 50-year-old woman, with a three-month-old baby on my lap, contemplating what to do first. Should I dye my hair, lose 10 pounds, put on makeup, or what? Since there was no solution for this predicament, I had to let him in and mask my obvious physical flaws by using my wit and sparkling personality. As sparkling as a frumpy, middle-aged babysitter can be, that is. While I was composing my game plan, "Mr.-I'm-glad-I-got-up-this-morning-and-have-this-great-job" came in and flashed his dazzling smile. After my computer difficulties were explained, he struts up the stairs and gets straight to his work. He trots down 10 minutes later, looks at me as if I fit the description of sex starved housewife in his code book, and states, "Lady, there is a dial tone on your phone."

Confidently, I ran up those steps, whipped that receiver to my ear, and sure enough heard a buzzing sound that sounded suspiciously like a dial tone. I can't believe this! I know that phone was malfunctioning all weekend and I have emails floating out there in space to prove it.

Just so the day would not be a total loss, I decided to make the best of a bad situation and spend time flirting with Mister Wonderful. As I sat there (stomach in, chest out) trying to look alluring, my two three-year-old toddlers woke up from their naps, came into the kitchen and stood guard on either side of me. *Get away kids, you bother me.*

Even though the preschool squad put a major crimp in my style of spending time with the Playboy of the Year, things were going pretty well. Social niceties were exchanged while comments about the weather and computer were bantered about. Propping my hands under my chin, I was gazing at his sparkling smile wondering why he didn't chuck this job to make toothpaste commercials, when the baby decided to regurgitate her lunch and spewed a wad of formula towards my handsome house guest.

Time stood still as we both watched this projectile make a perfect arch and land (plop) inches from that handsome devil's polished boots. Alas, the spell was broken. He swiftly flipped his sunglasses over his eyes, did an about face, and raced out the door mumbling something about checking the box at the pole.

A half-hour later, a phone call from the main office was received stating and I quote, "The problem has been checked and everything is functioning. **I repeat, there is absolutely no problem with your phone lines."**

For a week after this episode, things were going great as emails were flying back and forth at a rapid pace. Then an eerie silence prevailed. Did I offend, or what? There were no emails, no promos, nothing! Reluctantly, I connected my computer line to the phone outlet, and slowly lifted the receiver to my ear to hear, you guessed it, Complete Silence! Realizing that another call to Bell Tell would further tarnish my reputation with the men of the telephone union, I hesitated to report the problem. However, five minutes later, common sense prevailed as I reasoned that I am paying for a phone line that is not functioning. After all, isn't it my inalienable right to communicate?

So, I got on the horn, and before you know it, here comes old reliable (the bedraggled middle-aged man to whom I relate so well). I was apprehensive as he picked up the phone and relieved when he heard nothing. After deciding that yes, I do have a phone line problem and no, I am not one of those women aptly described in his manual, he left to check the wires at the pole.

Later that afternoon, Old Reliable and Mister Wonderful appeared together in the middle of my yard and shouted, "Lady your phone line was loose at the pole and is now fixed." For Pete's sakes did they think I was desperate enough to jump their bones if they came any closer? FYI boys, one of you is way too worn out, and the other is just a bit too polished for me to be interested.

I am happy to report that the above technical difficulties were finally resolved, my phone line functioned beautifully, and I was back in the email business again.

PART TWO:

Into the Thick of Things

10

Puddlemania

First the worst, second the best, third the golden bird. I'm not sure what fourth is, but it must be scary if Puddle's shows are any indication.

A year ago, my son resurrected his band, PUDDLE. I immediately sensed excitement, fame, a social life, and decided it would be in my best interest to ride the coattails of this exciting project. So, I approached the boss (my son) and asked if I could be President of Marketing. Ever the shrewd businessman, he stroked his chin and narrowed his eyes as he said, "Well I don't know." I then added the clincher, "I will work for free." Before the *ee* sound was out, I was hired and launched into the wonderful world of show business.

The job description included paying my way into all shows, selling the band's merchandise, and of course, buying as many beers as possible to demonstrate that Puddle fans are good for the economy of whatever bar decides to book them. This is my kind of job, alright.

(First the worst): As I said, the first show was the worst. Most of the crowd came to see another band and they were very Puddle unfriendly.

(Second the best): This show was at Pancho O'Hare's and we had fun! Puddle managed to attract 50 fans from days gone by, while the locals of the bar got into the action. They were clapping on the sidelines when a big guy, reminiscent of Gene-Gene the Dancing Machine from The Gong Show of the 80's, came shuffling across the floor. With a beer mug in one hand, a cue stick in the other and a baseball cap on his head, he got the music in him and started to dance to one of Puddle's original songs. Suddenly my daughter (by day a sophisticated middle school teacher, by night dancing queen) shimmied onto the floor and began doing the bump with Gene-Gene. Before long the whole place erupted as dancers and non-dancers alike joined in and began moving to the beat.

(Third the Golden Bird): The third show found us once again at Pancho O'Hare's. The advertised band cancelled, and Puddle was the surprise substitute. Not to worry, the President of Marketing was on the job. More Puddle fans joined fans from the cancelled band and newly recruited regulars from the bar. I even coerced my mother and a few close friends to attend. As I sat there performing my duties of selling merchandise and drinking beer, I glanced up to see dear old Mom being twirled back and forth between four dignified businessmen. *Mom*, I thought, *you have a bad knee and aren't supposed to be walking much less dancing. For Pete's sakes sit down.* I guess the music got to her and she could not stop her dancing feet. Encouraged by this overwhelming response, I could hardly wait for the next gig. That is why I am not sure how to describe this show.

Ronnie Mundis

Driving down a deserted dead-end street in the depths of the city, a biting chill shook my body warning me of the danger ahead. That feeling was validated as I walked through the door and was taken back 50 years to a 1940's setting where the bar regulars looked like they just got off work down in the coal mines. Some had no teeth, some had no hair, but they were all loud and outspoken. As I peeked into the next room, I noticed a bunch of men, old and young alike, pulling up their shirts and pointing to something on their chests. I don't know if it was chest hairs or piercings, but they were comparing something above their waists.

Before the decision of entering this testosterone domain was made, my husband appeared, shoved a beer in my hand, escorted me to a table and said, "Sit here while I play pool with **THE MEN**!" A half-hour later, he resurfaced with two Mexican gentlemen named Carmine and Miguel in tow, gave them each a beer, sat them next to me, and then left. After looking at them for a few minutes, my questions concerning the customs of Mexico prompted an interesting response. Carmine stated, "My wife, she die, I

It's Funny Because It's True

sad." While Miguel added, "Puddle iss good; yes, Puddle iss good." No matter what I asked, their responses remained the same leading me to believe that was the extent of their English. "My wife she die" was an interesting phrase. Come on guys lighten up, it's Saturday night and I am trying to have a Budweiser moment here. Unfortunately, unless I wanted to join the bare-chested men gathered around the pool table, I was stuck with Carmine and Miguel and their Mexican lingo.

As the music got louder, the Puddle fans gathered at one end of the bar, while the regulars contributed comments from their favorite bar stools, yelling critiques between songs. My son answered back and before you know it, whimsical quips were being exchanged and a comedy routine of sorts developed. Flanked by the Mexicans to my back, rowdy bar regulars to my right, Puddle fans to my left, and the band in front of me, I must admit this job was not as glamourous as I had hoped.

Next week we will be performing at a biker bar where Pagan motorcycle gang members are the bouncers. Oh well, That's Show Biz, Folks!

11

Fifty Something

This whole mess was Felicity's fault. Felicity, you know, the bewildered coed appearing on Channel 10 on Sunday nights who copes with one college dilemma after another.

On this week's episode, she had her golden mane of curly locks cut into an extremely short poodle style. You know what? It looked good, damn good! Therefore, the next day I raced to our local beauty shop and demanded, "Cut it off, cut it all off!" That cozy clipper just smiled as she raised her shears and cut and cut and then cut some more. Upon shampooing and fluffing it up a bit, I gazed in the mirror and saw a lovely young lady staring back at me. "Looking good girlfriend. You are looking *real* good!"

Ronnie Mundis

After singing the first two stanzas of "I Feel Pretty," accompanied by some nifty footwork, I stepped back to ponder the situation. While the face was youthful, this body would never do. I know – I'll whip it into shape by taking a two-mile walk around my neighborhood. Yes sirree, that is exactly what I need (A HEALTHY WALK). The wind was blowing, the sun was shining, and I felt great as I jogged down the hill at a brisk pace.

It seemed like a perfect day until I noticed the DO NOT ENTER sign blocking the exit leading home. Approaching two more exits and realizing they were also blocked by the boys in hard hats, I became concerned the girlfriends invited for lunch would arrive before the subs I forgot to order. Panicking, I rushed to the next corner and made a mad dash for the open alley before the men in the steel tipped boots arrived with their equipment and barriers. Launched into uncharted territory, my eyes cast about for something familiar when my foot tripped on the uneven sidewalk and I went down like a lead weight.

It's Funny Because It's True

There was absolutely nothing graceful about this situation. At the ripe old age of 55 years, I guess your equilibrium changes and what used to be a stumble easily righted, now turns into an out-and-out fall.

Two options came to mind as I approached the ground. I can go face first into the concrete, risking plastic surgery or, at least, painful dental work, or break my fall with my right hand. Before I knew it, my hand was down, and my body collapsed into a crumbled mess. Laying there watching my hand swell to four times its size, one thought came to mind. Getting to the doctor for medical treatment, you say? Certainly not! I was planning how to manipulate my swollen hand to drive to the local deli to buy those subs for lunch. It was now obvious that this fall had not only destroyed my hand, but must have rattled my brain as well.

After 10 painful days of watching my hand shrink down to just twice its normal size, I must admit that maybe a trip to the emergency room would have been wiser than having that fattening lunch.

Ronnie Mundis

Exactly two weeks after the mighty fall, black spots appeared on the fringe of my peripheral vision. It seemed to be something like my Great Grandma used to see when she would swat at nothing. Yes, now at the tender age of 55, I am seeing little fruit flies and I'm just a'swinging away. Attributing those spots as a side effect of my high blood pressure, I wasn't alarmed until shooting stars began to appear inside my head. Those stars sent a message to my brain that something dangerous was happening here and I needed to call my eye specialist and demand an appointment. My concern was validated by the response of "Get in here *Immediately!*"

Upon arrival, the head honcho, instead of the usual receptionist, greeted me at the entrance. He gently took my arm and slowly escorted me to a private room, leading me to believe that either this place is hard up for business, or I am in a lot of trouble here.

To make a long story short, I spent Halloween, not giving out candy as planned, but having laser surgery to correct a detached retina.

It's Funny Because It's True

This procedure, which involved 460 laser blasts to my eye, has affected my subconscious and explains the following reoccurring nightmare. I am ushered into the examining room by a familiar looking nurse. As I sit admiring the diplomas on the wall, a small Asian physician enters wearing western garb complete with Stetson, bandana, chaps and holster. She suddenly pulls out her laser gun, waves it in my face saying, "You need just a few more zaps, a few more." Then I hear a blood curdling scream and wake up in a cold sweat.

Today I was sitting in my living room remembering that one short month ago, I was feeling pretty good about myself. That was, of course, before I decided to take the infamous Healthy Walk. Now the hair is long, the eyes are tired, and the body is fat. I was examining my swollen hand with my one good eye when my daughter asked, "Hey Mom when are you going back to work?" To that I replied, "I am working, working hard to survive another day. Wait a minute, maybe I can be the poster child for Healthy Walks."

12

The Bridal Shower

As soon as my daughter said, "Mom, this would be the perfect house for my bridal shower," I knew what I had to do.

I told my realtor, "This is THE ONE! Put up the SOLD sign. I don't need to see the inspector's report, because any house that satisfies my daughter's discriminating taste is good enough for me." Thus, the 10-year search for our new domain ended and we were ready to plan our first social event.

Before the ink was dry on the settlement sheet, our little bride knew where her shower would be held. The only element of surprise would be when.

To obtain this goal, the following plan was developed: First, all the guests would gather at the daycare location about three miles away; Second, the groom and his best man would shuttle the guests to the party at least a half an hour before the scheduled event; Third, the Maid of Honor would deliver the bride at 2pm; and Fourth, everyone would party hearty. Yes, this was going to be a grand affair!

Confident that all was in order, I pictured myself relaxed and composed, dressed in Fashion Bug's finest, ladling sherbet-laced punch into fancy crystal cups as guests make affectionate comments about the lovely couple.

Of course, none of that happened. Instead it was total chaos! An hour before the designated start time, as I was about to jump in the shower, the groom called to inform me that he and his best man had been involved in a car accident. So, instead of chauffeuring the party goers, they were waiting for the police. Relieved that they were unhurt, I figured I could handle this glitch by calling The Maid of Honor and telling her the start time would be delayed. Unfortunately, her cell phone was not accepting calls, so unless I could get someone else to pick up the party goers, the Guest of Honor might arrive before her party guests. Since my other daughter was busy transporting people from **Our Side**, there was only one option left - ME. That's how, instead of lighting candles and making punch, I rushed out of my air-conditioned house in my sweatpants and sneakers and went to pick up the guests waiting to attend the party. To my surprise instead of finding the expected guests from **Their Side**, I found nobody (not one single soul).

Afraid that somehow the wrong date was put on **Their Side's** invitations, I panicked and called home. My angry husband answered, "Hurry home, there are a lot of people coming in the door, and I am not sure what to do." As the sweat poured off my brow, I calmly requested to speak to the groom's mother, who informed me that **Her Side** decided to ignore the shuttle plan and just come to my house. And, by the way, where was **My Side**? After composing myself by taking a deep breath, I replied, **"My Side** is arriving in 15 minutes because *they* know how to follow directions."

Hot and bothered, I trooped back home and was amazed to see only one unfamiliar car parked in my driveway. Knowing this car would ruin the surprise, I approached the guests from **Their Side** and politely asked, "Could whoever owns the green Taurus, please park it in the garage?" Then from a corner of the room, a senior citizen bellowed, "That car is just fine where it is and will remain right in that driveway!" Shocked at the audacity of this guest, I countered, "Excuse me, perhaps you ladies do not know who I am. I happen to be The Mother of The Bride." From the sofa there came a yell, "Yeah, well that and a dollar will get you a cup of coffee, honey."

Noticing that my husband was floating around the room pouring warm soda from a two-liter Pepsi bottle into small plastic bathroom cups, I used this as an excuse to gracefully exit to the kitchen to check on my punch.

What I found was a completely empty punch bowl. Now all my illusions of a perfect party were shattered. No lit candles, no sherbet-laced punch ladled into fancy crystal cups, and certainly no affectionate comments on the lovely couple. Undaunted I raced to make the punch and light my candles while smiling at my belligerent guests.

One-by-one, the people from **My Side** gathered in the kitchen to escape the tension coming from the people on **Their Side**. When the annoying owner of the Taurus entered to inform me, and I quote, "I am leaving now, as if anyone cares." I waved, grinned, and answered, "Thanks for coming and by the way don't let the door hit your rear end on the way out."

As you may imagine, we are all anxiously anticipating the wedding.

13

A Visit to the New House

Looking forward to enjoying a long-awaited day off over July 4th, I was surprised when Mom came to visit for the WHOLE WEEKEND. Understand - my mother does not just visit, SHE ATTACKS! Unfortunately, the person she attacks is, you guessed it, my better half. Okay, he is a bit of a slob and a procrastinator, but nobody is perfect, right? It would be bearable if she would stop shouting, "Oh my poor daughter!" while she was attacking.

Suffice it to say, due to my Mom's directions on home improvements, I now have towel racks and toilet paper holders in all three bathrooms. Pictures of all the kids are hung in the hallway, there is a gigantic painting of a blue cat on my dining room wall, new lamps are on both end tables, and a French Horn sprouting artificial flowers hangs beneath the family portrait.

For a reason, unbeknownst to modern man, the previous owner drilled two holes on the inside of the front door. Hardly noticeable to us, but they were a point of concern for dear old mom who, upon arrival, slapped a huge flower covered straw hat on the door to cover them. Now the holes are still there, but who cares? Since my decorating ability is limited and it makes her ever so happy, I gave her the go ahead because anything suits this Home Sweet Home.

When Hubby stopped hammering nails to bandage the blisters on his hands, the picture hanging marathon was over and Mom began her second phase of our home improvement by picking on our big old tom cat, Coors. Let me preface this by stating that Coors does not know he is a cat, but he is, in fact, a valued member of our family. His work here is to keep our bed warm, cuddling close at night, and bugging me for his daily rations at four o'clock in the morning. Therefore, when a strange person approaches

It's Funny Because It's True

telling him that he stinks and should eat down in the laundry room by his litter box, he does not handle it well. He has a panic attack, goes to the box in question and proceeds to have diarrhea over the sides, down to the floor. This emits a worse smell than his canned food did in the kitchen, and the debate about where the cat should eat and poop continues. Let's face it, do you want to eat in the bathroom? Obviously neither does Coors because when he saw his dish descend to the lower level of our house, he began to pace back and forth and refused to leave the bedroom. Refused, that is, until good old mom finished sweeping his hair off the chair in the living room and flipped the cushion. Then he majestically jumped up on that clean cushion, circled twice, gave a big old cat yawn, put his head down and went to sleep. The power struggle was on.

Needless to say, by Sunday, the situation was becoming tense as we had all the cleanup and fix-up activities we could stand. When Mom announced, "Boy, I bet you guys will be happy to see this old lady go home so you can get some rest," we wisely kept our comments to ourselves, nodded and smiled. With her luggage in hand and our tongues in our cheeks, we packed up her car, waved goodbye, and bid her a fond adieu.

My husband is still not speaking to me, but hey, until Tuesday, I was too busy hanging up my bathroom towels and filling my toilet paper dispensers to notice.

14

Pathmark Shoppers

Attention Pathmark shoppers! Attention! This common phrase aroused my interest as I thought a delicious Special to perk up another gloomy winter day was about to be announced. What a surprise when, instead of hearing about the Daily Deal, this statement followed: "We need your help. We are looking for an elderly gentleman with long gray hair and a large hat. He was last seen in the cereal aisle when he wandered away from his cart and disappeared. If you see someone fitting this description, please notify any Pathmark employee."

Suddenly the vision of a SWAT team of apron clad clerks descending upon this senior gentleman as he points his cane shouting,

"Dagnabbit you whippersnappers, unhand me – I just went to the freezer to get some ice cream!" popped into my head and caused me to burst out a squeal of laughter. Composing myself, I paid for my goods and went chuckling and snorting all the way to my car, displaying very inappropriate behavior for one a whisper away from her golden years.

Then a voice in my head announced, *You have really done it this time, and God is going to get you for it.* That is only a figure of speech, right? I mean I didn't believe God was actually going to get me or anything. That thought changed the next day when I was assaulted by my car door and sustained a massive head injury.

Two years ago, I took a healthy walk and ended up with a detached retina for my efforts. Since then, I have not taken any chances. Working out, jogging, walking, or swimming are not my cup of tea. Exercise-wise, I am aware that I am physically challenged and do nothing to encourage any injury to my accident-prone body. However, on this day, God was a little too clever for me. I cautiously opened the door to my parked car and prepared to enter when Whammo!! For no reason, the door swung out of control, slammed into my head, causing my glasses to get stuck in the middle of my forehead. When removed, a stream of blood gushed down my nose, slid off my chin onto my new winter jacket, causing an unsightly mess. Applying ice did stop the bleeding and swelling, however, the damage had been done. I now have a red scar on my forehead (very visible directly below the third eye), a severe headache, and a black puffy eye. To make matters worse, the right side of my body aches because it was jolted out of alignment.

This week after visiting my chiropractor to correct my posture, my eye doctor to see if my retina is still attached, and my primary physician for a prescription for pain medication, I reflected on the situation. This whole scenario began when I laughed at that little old man. "Lord I have seen the light and have decided to mend my wicked ways. Now stop it!!"

15

The Gold Watch

There was no excuse for the situation which had arisen at this time (absolutely no excuse). If I had not been lusting after a 14-carat gold watch all day, I would not have noticed what was on the woman's wrist three bodies ahead of me in the express lane at a local supermarket. There it was. A beautiful gold watch on a hand that kept going in and out of a lovely leather pocketbook. For 20 minutes I watched my coveted piece of jewelry dip and retrieve, dip and retrieve, as the woman in question attempted to pay for items, not covered by her food stamps, with rejected credit cards.

Curious to see who was attached to this timepiece, my eyes traveled from her manicured fingernails to her fingers over the watch up her arm to the top of her head. What did I see, you ask? Oh, just about $2,000 worth of genuine gold jewelry, that's all. Lo and behold, she had gold rings on every finger, three gold earrings in each ear, numerous gold chains around her neck, and that all important Gold Watch. It was disgusting!

As I stood there with a $15 Timex on my wrist, a wedding band on my finger, and cash in my pocket to pay for my vittles, Little Miss Food Stamp was decked out like a 14-carat gold Christmas Tree.

While waiting for the line to move, I decided to talk to the pleasant looking woman in front of me. Okay, so I may have begun my conversation with this line as an ice breaker: "That girl is wearing more gold jewelry than I will own in my lifetime, and, of course, she is paying with food stamps." To this that little lady replied, "Isn't that the truth! I wonder why she doesn't barter her pinky ring to pay for her goods, so we can get the hell out of here." Then we both laughed and talked about other things until the line began to move. After checking out, I headed quickly out of the store.

As I was loading my car, the roar of an engine followed by squealing brakes grabbed my attention. A large passenger van stopped three yards away, and a woman, who looked like the person in line in front of that lovely lady with whom I had such a pleasant conversation, emerged from her vehicle and was making a beeline towards little ol' me. Disgruntled, as I had just spent 50 minutes in an express lane to buy $10 worth of groceries, I prayed, "Please Lord deliver me from this fine woman." He answered, "No such luck, honey," as Big Bertha just kept a'coming my way.

All I could do was stare as she waddled closer and berated me for my discreet food stamp comment. "I wanna let you know that girl gets up and goes to work every day, every day of her life! So just shut your big ugly mouth!" A few choice expletives followed as she pounced back into her van and laid rubber on her way out of the lot.

Totally shocked, several clever replies, such as, "I go to work every day, too, and no one sings my praises," and "maybe she should buy less jewelry so she could pay for her groceries," came to mind. Wisely, I decided to keep my big ugly mouth shut and gazed in wonder at her retreating vehicle. It stands to reason that anyone who would wait outside in 95- degree weather for the sole reason of yelling at a total stranger may be a tad irrational and perhaps slightly unbalanced.

Determined to ignore absolutely everything that happened today, I quietly got into my car and began to drive away when paranoia set in. I imagined Big Bertha was on her cell phone calling the reserves with a description of my car and license number. Just in case, I ducked into the nearest phone booth and called home with this request, "Pull out the heavy artillery since I may have to make a run for the door when I get home." Thankfully, my daughter answered, "I have the garden hose ready in case of an attack and next time, please behave yourself, Mom."

16

Minding My Own Business

What is it with me and grocery stores? I go in to make a purchase and, for no obvious reason, someone starts shouting at me. It happened 20 years ago over a gold watch, and today, gosh darn, it happened again.

Here I am a quiet, pleasant looking senior citizen, with a big smile on my face, going into my local store to buy a party tray. There was a song in my heart and a skip in my step as I approached the deli counter and nothing, absolutely nothing, was going to ruin my good mood. Not when I picked number 79 and realized number 65 was being served, or when I noticed there was only one worker filling the orders, so customers would be waiting a longer time. I never flinched, but nicely positioned my cart in a half circle along with the other patrons, and waited patiently for my number to be called.

Abruptly, a baby's scream (a shrill, temper tantrum scream) disrupted the mood of this already edgy group. Tensions escalated as 10 more minutes passed with little progress in the deli department (we were now on number 70), and the noise from our screamer just got louder and louder. Taking a deep breath, I began to rub my forehead wondering why the parents of that child were not trying to quiet him. Certain that I never opened my mouth to express those thoughts, I was shocked when an irate young gentleman got in my face and began to shout, "That's right, lady it's a baby crying. That's what babies do, they cry."

A hush came over the crowd as I turned red and cast my eyes to the floor. Wait a minute. All I did was rub my forehead. I have no reason to be ashamed. In fact, he should be the one to apologize for upsetting all of us. Wisely I kept my mouth shut and diverted my gaze until this bully's number was called and he moved five feet away to the front counter.

Feeling a little safer, I turned to the person on my right and softly whispered, "Wow." She whispered back, "Honey you did not do anything wrong. This is just the world we live in now." Suddenly, Mr. Self-Righteous was back in my face shouting, "Lady, do you have a problem with the way my wife and I are raising our baby. Well do you?"

Knowing that question did not warrant a response, I continued to look at my cart as my body began to shake, and I am not going to lie, I did pee a little. Truth be told, I was scared! Suddenly, news headlines, "Tragedy today as a 70-year-old grandma was shot for rubbing her forehead while toddler screams," flashed before my eyes. I felt extreme panic and hoped for a miracle. My prayers were answered as the skies darkened and a heavy downpour provided the cover needed for me to run huffing and puffing to my car.

Later as I merged onto the highway, memories of the happy-go-lucky person I was that morning flashed through my mind. I had turned into a disgruntled, hot mess. The skip in my step had disappeared and the lyrics of "Happy Days Are Here Again," the song in my heart from earlier, was replaced by "The Rainy-Day Blues."

Upon pulling into the driveway of my destination, the license plate on the car in front of me read, "NRAS4U2." Oh no, no, no NRAS not 4 me 2 but those exitS R definitely 4 me. So, instead of going to the party, I turned around and drove home.

17

The Family Pet

Two months after our beloved guinea pig crossed over to that great forest in the sky, my husband gave our children The No More Family Pets Speech. With everyone in agreement, it was settled. There would be no more pets in this family. That is why today, when I looked out my window and saw a mangy ball of dirty yellow fur eating something from my everyday stoneware, I was determined to find out who was feeding this thing. After my youngest daughter confessed and promised no more food would be leaving our house under any circumstances, I was surprised when the next day, I saw another plate outside with residue that closely resembled last night's leftovers. This time, my oldest daughter was the culprit. Another stern talking to resulted in more promises given, so I thought that was the end of the conversation. I was confident that this matter was resolved, until the following evening when I caught my spouse serving healthy choices to our uninvited guest. The message was clear: this household was ready for a new family pet. Thus, on August 7, 1992, a skinny, dirty yellow cat was welcomed into our humble abode and affectionately named COORS. Coors was a mature tom, no cuddly, kitten stuff for him, and, as such, he stayed to himself.

Things were clicking along just fine until two weeks later when a strange odor oozed from the corner of the family room. Oh No! Kitty had an accident. As designated Domestic Engineer, I took the situation in hand. After words and meows were exchanged, the cat, cat food, litter and litter box were dumped out by the trash can. Proud of my assertive behavior in taking charge of a messy situation, I informed everyone that as of today there would be no more family pet. Surprised when, instead of a pat on the back, hubby announced, "When the litter box is returned to its rightful place, I will return," and

It's Funny Because It's True

then slammed the door and left. Two hours later, after surviving hateful looks from my girls and still no husband in sight, I realized I may have acted a tad hastily and returned the litter box to its rightful place along with the cat food, cat toys and Mister Coors himself.

As promised my husband returned and life went on as usual, or so I thought. The next week when arriving home, we found a parchment on the kitchen table titled, "The Family Pet Contract." It contained the following conditions: 1. I am not a kitten so there will be none of that cuddly, mushy kitten talk; 2. I am not now and never will be a plaything for those little creatures you call daycare children who run around this household all day long; 3. I only eat USDA Prime meat and 100% whole milk heated to room temperature; 4. I must be allowed to go outside any time of the day or night with no judgment concerning my activities; 5. Since I am finicky, I expect three or four choices for my dinner which I may or may not eat; and 6. Of course, it goes without saying, that litter box in the trash incident must never ever happen again. Provided all the above terms are met, I will condescend to live here as your family pet. Then we put our John Hancocks on the decree dated August 25th, 1992, and Puddy Tat was embraced as a new member of our family.

Since he stayed upstairs most of the time and only graced us with his presence once or twice a year, I rarely saw our feline friend. Unfortunately, the once or twice happened to be when the daycare inspector came to check my state food program. As soon as the doorbell announced her arrival, Coors would prance down the steps and jump onto a kitchen chair in time for our hearty lunch. "Oh my (chuckle, chuckle), I cannot imagine where that cat came from," I uttered through my clenched teeth as I pushed him off that chair. "Really, he never comes down here at all." I almost had her convinced that this was a one-time occurrence until our conversation was interrupted by uncontrollable giggling of children. They were throwing bits of fish sticks in the air as Coors leaped up, retrieved the food in mid-stride and gobbled the offering. "Tsk, tsk," sighed the inspector as she gave me 10 demerits for not only having an animal in the eating area, but also distracting entertainment at mealtime as

It's Funny Because It's True

well. Then Coors retreated to his cave upstairs and did not show his fur again until six months later when another inspection was due. Thus, years went by as we coexisted in relative comfort until we moved to a new house.

Everyone worried that our beloved pet would feel uncomfortable in these unfamiliar surroundings and run away. But once adjusted, he made this castle on top of the hill his own. At our old house, he was merely a silent presence, however, in this new environment, our quiet tabby turned into a highly vocal personality. What used to be quiet, calm mornings were now turned into a disaster by the following routine: beginning at 5AM, ol' green eyes worked the hall outside our bedroom door like it was the stage of The Grand Old Opry. He did not meow sweetly but proceeded to belt out a solo that sounded like, "mayrow, mayroow, maroonie, madagroonie, maurow!" This went on forever until the door was slammed in his face. Annoyed, our off-key singer scratched frantically at the closed entrance until it was opened so we could clearly hear his finale. At 5AM, it sure sounded clear to me. At the end of this performance,

Puddy sauntered into the room and leaped onto our bed in one graceful swoop. If perchance any part of my anatomy was close to my hubby's right hand, ping! A sharp claw applied steady pressure on the offending appendage until blood flowed, and I rolled out of the way. Then with his spot secured, the head rubbing portion (which involved 10 minutes of vigorous rubbing and loud purring), continued followed by the water lapping segment. Since all that singing and purring worked up a mighty thirst, a cup of water always sat on the shelf at the top of our bed. After all, one could not expect our little opera star to walk all the way into the kitchen for his refreshment. Wouldn't that be animal cruelty?

This day, due to my spring-cleaning efforts, his cup was missing. That caused our shocked and bewildered little lion to stare at my hubby as if to say, "What, no water?! (Chop! Chop! Peon!!). Instantly, my better half scurried out of bed and reappeared seconds later with a cup of sparkling spring water with an ice cube floating in it. Now at 5:30AM, the water lapping part of this routine has caught my attention, and out of the corner of my blood shot eye, I must

It's Funny Because It's True

applaud the master as he orchestrates his daily fiasco. Finally, having quenched his thirst, our super star slinks to the end of our bed, circles twice, and collapses into a deep sleep. Ah! Silence, now I can get a few more winks. Ring! Ring! The alarm clock signaling the start of a new day pulls me out of bed, but by the time I stumble into the kitchen, my better half is reading the funnies to none other than, you guessed it, our pampered Kumba. On this day he was perched on my chair causing me to lose my temper and yell, "Young man, get out of my chair this instant!" Young man? For Pete's sakes, I am talking to a cat here. Hubby snickers. Coors looks at me and snorts, as he jumps down and goes back to my bed for *my* beauty sleep.

Other than this annoying morning routine, Coors was a cherished addition to our family. Today, as usual, I let him out and expected to see him under his favorite bush by the back door when I called, but he was nowhere in sight and the hunt began. After hours spent searching and anguishing over his whereabouts, we found our little Man's Best Friend 360 feet away on the side of a highway.

Ronnie Mundis

We buried our Pudd on top of the hill where he truly remains King of This Mountain. One day, you decided it was time to leave, but my dear friend, we were not ready to let you go.

PART THREE:

Poetic Pause

18

Stella's Poetry Corner
Verses by my Mother-in-Law, Stella Mundis

These are a young mother's poems about marriage, children and life in the 1950s and 1960s.

Summer Breeze

So sweet does the evening breeze blow
At the end of a summer day.
The light is gone, the fireflies glow.
The heat is held at bay.

Ronnie Mundis

Rowing

At Lake Bistanneau you secured a boat
And asked me would I ride.
The sun was high and very hot
And heat waves pressed from every side.
We rowed among the lily pads
And touched the lily flowers.
We passed beneath the Cyprus Giants
And saw the mossy flowers.

We drifted down the channel stream
Steering clear the locust trees.
We picked huge Magnolia blossoms
And made white garland leis.

We gazed at our reflections
Before the two oars fell.
You were a Southern Gentleman
I was a Southern Belle.

It's Funny Because It's True

Five

I'll whisper a secret in your ear.
For you alone, My Mother Dear.

I'll grow up this very year
And marry you, My Mother Dear.
I'll always stay so close and near
To keep you company, Mother Dear.

I'll be a man, not shed a tear.
For I am five, My Mother Dear.

Mrs. Murnane

I met an angel on her way
To cheer a shut-in one dreary day.
She was old and she wore black.
Burden on burden had bent her back.
But on her face was a happy smile,
And under her feet a traveled mile.
I pity the many who never knew
An angel had passed when they saw you.

Ronnie Mundis

Spring Storm

Wind and rain sweep through the trees,
Cooling the cobbled street.
Trucks and cars must all beware
Their slippery beat.

Storms fret and brew in the springtime,
Slowing the hurried pace.
Of man and beast and engine
Around this busy place.

Easter Bunny

I knew that I would rue the day
That Easter Bunny came to stay.
He brought a duck for good old measure.
They've taken away all my leisure.

I feed and water and clean my floor,
And guard them when they're near the door.
The kids take Harry and Donald to heart.
But I'll be glad when they depart.

It's Funny Because It's True

All Gone

A little child will close his eyes
And say, "You can't catch me."
He thinks that he has disappeared
Because he cannot see.

Johnny's Truck

Johnny got a new red truck
Down at the 5 and 10.
He drove it up the stair rail
And how those wheels could spin!
He cautiously crossed the one-way street,
The truck held way up high.
His little voice changed all the gears
For people passing by.
That truck has travelled farther
And carried greater loads
Than all the trucks that travel
Upon the super roads.

Ronnie Mundis

The Lightning Bug

The lightning bug with his blinking light
Suddenly appears on a warm June night.
As dusk turns into inky shadows,
He blinks his light upon the meadows.
A guiding glimpse from his flashing beam
Shows clear his way, it does seem.
But where he's going and hoping to find
Is a deep, deep mystery to my mind.
And the secret of his electric light
Is puzzling as the dark of the moonless night.

Hunt

To walk in the woods in the bottomland
And hunt for the start of Spring.
As children we went there hand in hand.
Spirits did take wing.

It's Funny Because It's True

Teddy Bears and Little Boys

Teddy was the bad guy
and Johnny threw him in jail.
Except it was the vestibule and
Joey went his bail.
I speck that Teddy was shot
a hundred times or more.
And buried right on boot hill,
right behind the door.
Underneath the table
was another resting place
For the two little good guys are now
trying to save face.
The house was a shambles,
when the smoke cleared away.
So we put up the cap guns
and Teddy for today.

PART FOUR:

Later On

19

The Noodle Gobbler

It is that time of year again (The Daycare Continuing Education Credit time of year). That is when all childcare providers in the State of Delaware go in search of getting those all-important credits, to enable them to watch little Sammy and Susie for another 365 days or face rejection at the licensing bureau. Since I have a degree in Special Education, ran my own state sponsored school for academically challenged children for three years, raised four children of my own, and provided care for the youth of The Blue Hen State for the past 10 years, I may be a tad sarcastic and feel certain exemptions should be in order. After all, how much more can be discovered concerning children ages six weeks to five years? Same stuff, different course titles. Can this be another money-making scheme? Please say it isn't so.

In preparation for these so-called classes, I am sitting in front of a mirror practicing nodding my head and smiling to show agreement with any stupid comment the instructor utters. Last year, I was lucky enough to have a realistic teacher who acknowledged she was a burnt-out provider. She even looked burned out and sometimes even frowned. Thus, she now teaches. It was a great class with a lot of useful information. She even admitted to putting a sheet on a table and letting the kids play tent all day. Yeah, that's the stuff childhood memories were made of back in the day when kids had imaginations and did not need adults to entertain them. Alas, there was no such luck this year.

The only instructor teaching a 12-credit course within a 15-mile radius was Bubbling Betty. You know, the type who always smiles, speaks softly, and never loses her temper. Never loses her temper, that is, unless someone disagrees with her. This was a little-known fact that I discovered the hard way. I have been to enough of these classes to know the cardinal rule is never, *ever* disagree unless you want the three-hour session extended to three-and-a-half-hours. So, I paste a smile on my face, nod my head and, along with the other fine daycare professionals, grin and bear it.

The first two classes went great! I smiled at the comment that all children are natured the same way. I nodded at the idea that boys are more aggressive and physical than girls is just a myth. I smiled and nodded along with the group when Betty explained her lunch time policy was letting children who are finished eating leave the table to do an activity, while other children continue to sit and finish their meal. I scanned the crowd for a reaction to that ridiculous suggestion because common sense tells you that when one child leaves the table, they all want to leave, resulting in a chaotic situation. Surprisingly, nobody flinched and just kept a'grinning and a'nodding.

This nodding and grinning ended abruptly when Bubbly announced, "You care providers should do homework with your after-school care students before their parents pick them up. Surely you cannot expect these tired parents to go home, cook, clean and supervise homework." That was the final straw!! I opened my mouth and was not about to close it until I had my say. "Excuse me, I believe we are the *Care* Providers. Thus, we provide *care*. They are the *parents* and they provide the *parenting*. In my dictionary, homework falls under the category of parenting. If I remember correctly, putting those funky words into short sentences and the dreaded times table memorizations for second and third graders is a tedious process. Yes, I am absolutely sure homework is a parenting thing."

My comment received a frowny face from Betty, even though exclamations of, "You go girl!" and "Oh yeah, that's right!" arose from the crowd. Unfortunately, Betty was not so bubbly when someone proceeded to burst her bubble. I thought my suggestion was ignored until the end of the class when I realized the consequences of disagreeing with the master.

It's Funny Because It's True

What did she do, you ask? Well, she criticized my Noodle Gobbler, that's what she did. For a class assignment, I had submitted a color recognition activity that involved different colored elbow macaroni and peanut cans decorated in corresponding colors. The kids could feel the noodles, pick them up and drop them into matching colored containers. This activity involves small muscle and visual coordination, thus, these canisters were cleverly called Noodle Gobblers. An outstanding project especially compared to ones like paper hearts with accordion legs sticking out of the heart head and other unacceptable ideas.

Bubbly just loved my idea until we had the homework discussion. Then at the end of class, for no apparent reason, she blurted out, "By the way I think coffee beans are a better material for textile stimulation than dumb old macaroni, and they smell better, too." To that I responded, "Not to three-year-olds they don't. You show me a toddler who likes the smell of coffee and I'll show you one scary kid. Plus, you will have beans stuck up noses, going into mouths and ears and coming out covered with mucus, saliva and ear wax. These very expensive beans will then have to be discarded. Thank you very much. I shall now take my leave as I have expressed myself sufficiently for one night and feel it is time to go."

I may be excusing myself from this fine profession any day now as Bubbly has probably alerted the Licensing Inspector and things could get ugly. Oh well there is always the "Big C" (Corporate America). I am sure there is a fine position just waiting in a corporate establishment for an outspoken, innovative person like myself.

20

Corporate America

I have had enough! I am done! Pushed that one step too far and am not going to take it anymore. I am retiring my apron, uniform and pen as my waitressing days are over! Upon hearing that a new credit card operation in town was looking to hire people with food service experience, I decided to grab my chance and head into the great unknown world of Corporate America. Visions of paid sick days, vacation days, regular breaks and holidays appeared as a positive option to my career-changing decision.

Upon arriving for the interview, I was disappointed to learn that only part-time positions were available, and some of those desired benefits were not included. However, one must start somewhere, and I was determined to make a go of this opportunity. Even though the starting salary was half of what I was used to making, there was that prospect for advancement and less wear and tear on my aging body to consider. So, start up those engines and full steam ahead!

My first opportunity for success was working in the Security Department where people call when their cards are lost or stolen. It was a simple task to close the compromised account, alert the authorities for possible fraud and issue a new card with a different account number. This was a fun four-hour shift including a fifteen-minute paid break, and I was loving every minute of it. Soon it became apparent that my six-dollar hourly wage for twenty hours a week was not working for our family budget, so a move to a full-time position was my only recourse.

A week before moving up that corporate ladder, I received a call from a sweet lady named Edith. Upon hearing her sad tale of losing her dearly beloved husband, and how much she appreciates this credit card as it provides her with the ability to pay for her one luxury of a monthly shampoo and set, I did the unthinkable. Instead of transferring her to Correspondence where they would close the account, I said, "Edith, let me tell you how this works. On the one hand, I can transfer you to another department where they will request a copy of hubby's death certificate, promptly determine your income is not sufficient, and close your account. Then you can say goodbye to those hair appointments you love so much. On the other hand, this conversation never took place and you can just continue paying your bill every month and no one will be the wiser. What do you want to do?" She promptly hung up, only to call back five minutes later declaring, "I never spoke to you, you never spoke to me, and God bless you." That, my friends, is how to retain a client with excellent customer service. Not to worry, I was already moving on to bigger and better adventures in a department labeled Correspondence.

This branch proved to be a little more difficult as it involved handling charge disputes through the mail as email was not commonly used yet (prehistoric times). This policy had a time limit for the card holder to mail in evidence to support their disagreement. It was the representative's responsibility to follow up to obtain the required documentation and then transfer the information to the appropriate office. If you failed to follow up in a timely fashion, you would receive a reprimand which would influence the amount of your pay raise at your yearly review. All was well until Corporate decided to demand mandatory overtime. Now we reps were required to process new case disputes instead of using that time to follow up on our existing cases thus, adding to our follow-up folder, which we had no time to address. Subsequently, everybody received a bad desk review and a lower pay raise. As I watched my fellow workers grinning and nodding at this ridiculous, self-defeating policy, flashbacks to my daycare classes appeared and doubts about my business success surfaced. Not exactly the utopia I had pictured.

The only other option left to increase my salary was to explore the suggestion box incentive program. The one where cost saving ideas, if implemented, would reap a financial reward. I came up with several good proposals for form letters. My proposals involved inserting the required dates and documents needed on blanks on a pre-written letter that would appear at the click of the computer key instead of typing the same information over and over. This procedure would save employee time, which could be used to follow up on those dispute issues. My form letter idea was submitted and rejected. Rejected, that is, until I transferred to another department. Then the Assistant Supervisor submitted my idea under her name, received the monetary reward and was praised at our monthly meeting. Suddenly waitressing, where more productivity equals more money, did not seem like such a bad deal, and the idea of going back to that line of work was considered.

Determined to get my coveted two-week paid vacation for the first time in my life, I decided to hang in for another three months and moved to a subdivision called Customer Service. As I had dealt with this department for the last year and a half working in both Security and Correspondence, I knew just about everything that was involved. Nonetheless, as a new hire in this department, Corporate decided going through training two hours a day for two weeks to learn what I already knew was appropriate. Alrighty then! I was delighted to log off my computer in Correspondence (leave those messy disputes behind), and go into the training room and learn to do what I had been doing for the past year.

Maybe I did ruffle the feathers of a few supervisors as I jokingly announced that I was going to the training room now to learn what I already know, and waved at my co-workers on my way. This stuffy atmosphere brought out the devil in me. Some of my comments, although funny, were a little inappropriate. I was having a ball learning what I already knew and getting paid for it. I might still be working at that institution but alas, all good things must come to an end.

One day a restaurant owner who had been a regular customer of mine in days gone by when I worked at an upscale establishment, recognized my name on an old application and called with an offer that I could not refuse. I used my hard-earned two weeks paid vacation as my two-week notice, which no one tried to talk me out of and was eagerly accepted.

On my last day, as I was going towards the exit, I noticed all the supervisors and assistants had big smiley faces as they stood and waved. Thinking this was a marvelous sendoff, showing their appreciation for my competent work and innovative suggestions, I was charmed. Charmed, that is, until I heard rumblings of, "Good riddance!" and "Just not corporate material."

This was my experience working in Corporate America folks. I am happy I was able to move on, and I never looked back.

21

The Eviction

Soon after my husband left for work, the County Sheriff called and advised that time was up! Unless we could meet at 1PM today to follow through with the long-awaited eviction of one of our tenants, our court order would become invalid and we would have to go through the whole legal process again. Knowing this would involve another two months of court dates, with no rent in sight, and remembering how calm our last eviction was, I volunteered to meet the Constable and execute the order.

Six months ago, this procedure took a mere 30 minutes to complete. First, we showed up at the appropriate time. Second, we introduced ourselves to a tall, well-built, fine looking lawman with a six shooter on his hip and a taser under his vest. Then, without incident, he approached the empty house, changed the locks, and presto - we regained possession.

Since the tenants in this case had been given plenty of notice (at least three months), I anticipated a similar outcome. What could possibly go wrong? I only had to drive to the correct address and do the following: 1. Meet the robust, mean-looking Sheriff; 2. Check to make sure the house is empty. If not, stand outside with him until the tenants move; 3. Secure the windows and doors; and 4. Wait inside until my husband arrives to install a new lock. This is surely a walk in the park for the mean landlady and would finally rid us of our tenant from hell.

One day, exhausted from showing the property and tired of looking at unacceptable applications, I was swayed by a lovely smile and sweet voice and decided to rent to a pleasant, unqualified person. This was a hasty decision that I would later regret. After receiving many appreciative hugs, praises from heaven and alleluias, we signed on the dotted line and entered a friendly landlord/tenant relationship. Six months later, it all fell apart.

First, she bought a used car and then could not work because the used car salesman assaulted her. Apparently, my soft-spoken evangelist returned her purchase in such a way that instead of receiving a refund, she received a sound thrashing. Of course, she could not function while she was waiting for her case to prove she developed debilitating injuries. Therefore, she did not work or pay her rent for three months. I never believed the whole used car extravaganza and was shocked when the case was settled, and the full rent was paid two days before we were scheduled to evict. After this, there were numerous deaths in her family, severe asthma attacks, and the perennial female problem excuses to validate her tardy payment history.

One time she called and informed us that water was leaking from the pipe under her kitchen sink and her toilet was broken. We arrived to discover the pipe had been completely removed causing water to pour directly onto the bottom of the cabinet and the toilet bowl, not the tank, was shattered into 50 pieces. My husband and I stared at her in disbelief while she stood there with a blank look exclaiming that everything in the house just suddenly fell apart. Therefore, when she informed us that shortly after being released from rehab and finally returning to her job, she had been injured yet again when a bookcase fell on her, we seized the opportunity to rid ourselves of this accident prone, litigious renter.

    I arrived at the designated time and looked forward to intimidating our squatters with the presence of Wyatt Earp by my side. I sashayed to the Sheriff's car with a confident grin on my face, extended my hand to welcome a grim hombre and was startled when a petite lady in dress blues emerged from that official sedan. What is this?! Instead of Wild Bill I have one of the Lollipop Kids from the Wizard of Oz to assist me! Not quite as effective as I had hoped, however, a Sheriff is a Sheriff, and I do have the law and that all important six shooter on my side. So, let's do this!

It's Funny Because It's True

As we approached the house, we were surprised to hear laughter and music coming from within. Slowly, my disheveled tenant appeared with a surprised look on her face. I peeked inside and instead of seeing an empty living room with boxes packed, I observed a room full of furniture filled with men holding beer cans and eating potato chips. It seems that while I was agonizing over this eviction, my tenant was throwing a beer guzzling, chip dipping affair.

This was the last straw! I turned to that little Sheriff, pounded my left fist into my right palm and proclaimed, "I want them out!" Hearing this, my renter, a six-foot-tall woman with hair askew (definitely a bad bedhead day), rushes from her house crying, "Oh no, please no, we have an agreement that you will wait until I receive my new settlement."

Suddenly out of nowhere a crowd forms and my tenant's mom, who is sporting a Pippy Longstocking hairdo with ponytails sticking from every angle of her head, joins the crowd and chants, "Oh no, please don't make us go."

The Sheriff then asks, "What do you want to do?"

Again, I shook my fist and shouted, "I want them out!" Reluctantly, my fearless law enforcer said, "Okay then." She straightened fully into her four-foot frame, squinted her eyes as she glanced up two feet into Baby Huey's face and began to shake her finger as far as she could reach towards the gentle giant. Waving that small finger is not threatening anybody, so I patiently waited for the big guns to come out. Surprisingly, instead of showing her Colt 45, our little Miss Constable begins to laugh uncontrollably.

I had to take the situation in hand, walk the Sheriff to her car, and inform her that we were not being taken seriously and inquire about her instruments of violence. I mean where was that six shooter, the billy club, the semi-automatic? Show me something that will make this crowd sit up and take notice or, at least, stop dipping those chips. Unfortunately, the new landlord/tenant policy prohibits the use of weapons of any kind and now besides having the smallest Sheriff on the force, I do not even have an artillery at my disposal. What could we do but link arms, take a deep breath, and throw ourselves back into the fray?

Not to worry, I am informed that my tenant is awaiting a call from her boss to clear up this matter. Since we all know that no supervisors ever answer their phone, I smugly agree to wait 10 minutes before proceeding. Lo and behold, nine minutes later I am talking to a compassionate administrator, who informs me that yes, a bookcase did fall, caused a severe injury, and that a settlement would be coming. She followed with, "Could you please, please wait and not put these fine people out on the street?"

By now, the crowd outside has formed into a circle as they continue to chant, "Oh no, please don't make us go." The beer drinkers are partying louder, and my pint-sized enforcer informs me that regretfully, she must leave for another appointment. Before the Reality TV crew shows up with their cameras and microphones, I half-heartedly agree, "Okay you can stay." Hearing this, Pippy shouts, "Thank you, thank you. Let's all have a group hug." As the Sheriff slowly backs away, I pull her into the circle where we all, exhausted from chanting and laughing, experience a big old bear hug.

To this day, five years later, our tenant from hell is still with us. We may as well adopt her. Since then she only has a broken steel door and a few cracked windows to her credit, has obtained a pit bull named Diamond, a boyfriend named Bruce, and lost her Uncle What-Not (that's another story). She is presently pursuing a lawsuit against the local hospital for breaking her foot when she went in for knee surgery. On a lighter note, the events of that day are known far (as far as the Sheriff's office) and wide (as wide as the neighborhood) as The Most Memorable Eviction Ever.

22

Throwback Holiday

I do not know what is different this holiday season, but it is Thanksgiving, and I am not feeling it. Perhaps the chaos of dealing with destructive, ambivalent tenants for the past year may be contributing to my less than cheerful mood.

In April, after reviewing several rental applications, I decided to lease one of our houses to a girl who met our criteria of being employed and having a reliable rental reference. Since I pride myself as being a keen judge of character, I just knew I had chosen the perfect tenant. Unfortunately, two weeks after she moved in, she quit her job, invited her boyfriend over for the weekend, had her head slammed through a wall, and was threatened by a gun.

After the smoke cleared, the squad of six police cars left with the boyfriend in tow, and the ambulance spirited her away for treatment, I returned home to have a stiff drink and rethink my judgment abilities.

Good news! The next day we received a phone call informing us that our tenant from hell, whom we had been trying to get rid of for the past nine years, had moved. It seems that upon receiving her recent court order to vacate, she decided to avoid the drama of eviction and opted to leave under her own steam. Then she called to thank us for being such wonderful landlords, promised she would pay what she owed when she got her lawsuit settlement from The Dollar Store and insisted that we not bother returning her security deposit. What a great gal!

First, we were delighted to get our house back, but then saddened because her absence was like losing a needy relative. That feeling quickly changed to anger after we saw the condition of the house and realized that she did not choose to leave for our benefit, but because she could not stomach staying there another day. Apparently over the last six years as I was whimsically writing and mailing my newsletters out to elicit a chuckle or two, she was busy destroying her dwelling.

As soon as I entered this abode, an odoriferous wave of heavy cigarette smoke and accumulated dirt filled my nasal passages, causing my eyes to water, my throat to close, and my feet to rapidly carry me outside. I grabbed my unsuspecting husband's hand and pulled him over the threshold so he could witness the disaster that closely resembled "The Amityville Horror!"

All of the interior doors were hanging by one hinge, roaches ran amuck, the stove was missing, numerous holes of all shapes and sizes graced the walls, the door jams and baseboards were either broken or removed, the heater was in pieces, the back door hung ajar, the windows were broken, the floors were filthy, the remaining tiles had deep ruts carved into them and the back yard looked like a petrified forest. Wow! Who could have done all this damage? Surely not the pleasant lady who gave me those big old Christmas hugs and had the following answering machine message: "Praises go up and blessings come down. God loves you and have a good day." Did aliens take her away and replace her with the Tasmanian Devil or what?

Realizing that no sane human being could do this much damage one minute and present herself as a God-fearing person the next, we cautiously drove home to develop a game plan. Before we could regroup, there was a knock at the door where our friendly mail carrier presented us with a registered letter from yet another one of our marvelous tenants. It appears this dastardly duo, a couple I rented to six months ago, were ready to strike again.

On July 1st, 2008, using my keen character assessing abilities, I rented a home to a lovely couple who were gainfully employed, had no garnishments on their wages, and presented several outstanding rental references. Upon signing the lease, their statement of: "We are going to be the best tenants you people ever had," validated my decision. A month later the worst nightmare of our 20-year landlording career began. Following the manual of *How To Be Evicted For Dummies*, they proceeded to move another family into their unit, have loud parties, leave their young children (2 under the age of 5) home alone, and acquire two mean pit bulls, who were left outside every day between the hours of 2am and 4am to agitate the neighbors. So instead of the best, they became the worst tenants we ever had.

Before *America's Most Wanted* charged us with harboring a national nuisance and put us on **The List**, we had to act. Therefore, on November 1st, we combined forces with the Sheriff and the SPCA to restore peace to the neighborhood by escorting those offenders far, far away.

Within the next two weeks, we complied with The Landlord Tenant Code's requirements by assessing the damages they incurred and sent them a security deposit letter. Apparently, they did not care for our assessments and were now, with the help of the free legal aid system of the fine State of Delaware, suing us for their pain and suffering. That's right, their pain and suffering for having to live in our house for four months free!

Perhaps the above events contributed to my lackluster attitude as things did not seem quite right this turkey holiday. Although all the fixings were bought in a timely fashion, the preparation proved to be a real struggle. First the pumpkin for the pies burned and fell onto the bottom coil of my brand-new electric stove, emitting a pungent smell throughout the kitchen. Then the microwave died followed by the turkey bag exploding causing greasy turkey juice to cover the oven, the floor and the buffet table. I cleaned the oven, the kitchen floor, and the table while my husband continued cooking and creating more messes. Hence began a conflict over absolutely everything. Nothing suited. The table was not in the right position, the chairs were crooked, wrong tablecloths, my cute turkey and pumpkin salt and pepper shakers were replaced by a wooden pepper mill and a large container of Morton's salt. When I noticed my Grandmother's beautiful antique butter dish was replaced by a plastic plate with day old toast crumbs sticking in the butter, I exploded. Shouting, "Enough already!" Then I left the house and drove away venting about this horrible day.

Suddenly my eyes were drawn to something written on the rear window of the car in front of me. It looked exactly like my name, so I drove closer to get a better view and read the following script: "In memory of my loving sister, Veronica." Hello, I am the loving sister, Veronica, and I am still very much alive making wonderful memories, thank you. My bad mood instantly lifted as I drove home to enjoy a delicious Thanksgiving dinner.

23

The Secret

The Secret, The Secret! What is this thing called The Secret? I turn on Montel and there it is, switch to Oprah and I see it again, while the local news features the same information. Dismissing it as the latest motivational pish-posh, I walked to my mailbox and there it was staring back at me. Apparently, my aggressively positive sister was trying to push me onto the right path and sent it my way. The instructions given were to just pop this into your DVD player and wait for it to change your life. Seems like a simple enough directive to achieve all my hopes and dreams.

Unfortunately, after 10 minutes of watching a truly monotonous presentation, I dozed off and woke up to music announcing the final credits. Incapable of absorbing this information and finding no room for it in my junk drawer, that DVD was casually tossed on the kitchen table where my youngest daughter spied it and, with my blessing, whisked it away.

This interaction was forgotten until a week later when my little chick wanted to leave the nest and was applying to rent her own apartment. Knowing that she had good credit but only a part-time job and no rental history, I figured that a disappointing experience would surely follow. However, years of being a mom taught me to keep my mouth shut and wait for her to come to me for advice. At the end of the month she did come to me alright. But – instead of advice, she asked to borrow our truck to move her stuff into a pretty nice apartment. That's just beginner's luck, I thought. However, now a year later after observing her switch from one job to another, with a better environment and pay raise each time, buy herself a house, and begin two internet businesses, I have to admit there may be something to The Secret phenomenon.

It's Funny Because It's True

Upon reading the short version of this process in *The Secret for Dummies Cliff Notes*, I understood this system a little better. You just think positively about something you want, throw those vibes into the universe, and, presto! you get your wish.

First on my list was a desire to communicate with people I have not heard from in a while. Positive, positive vibes go! An hour later - Ring! Ring! My son who lives one mile away, whom I have not heard from in a month, calls and asks me to come over and visit. After that pleasant interlude - Ring! Ring! My cell phone ushers in my other son from Florida whom I have not heard from in three months. Arriving home after completing a lovely conversation with him - Ring! Ring! A call comes on my house phone from a friend I have not heard from in six weeks. Wow, this Secret thing is powerful stuff, but can it withstand the pressure of a really tough situation?

The next day was rent collection day, when inevitably most of our tenants are short on their rent. Unable to endure hearing any more of their excuses, I am going to utilize my new Secret attitude and picture everyone coming to their doors with their full rent in hand. Guess what? It worked! Not only was I greeted with the full rent but also smiley faces as they paid their water balances too.

Another opportunity to test this system came the following week when I bought 50-50 tickets at a local social function. Instead of picturing myself as a loser, I sat through the presentation silently composing my acceptance speech. Then when my number was called, I calmly walked up on stage to claim my prize. Those winnings coming home encouraged my skeptical husband to pop in that video, sit up, and pay attention.

While he was either gazing at the TV or sleeping, I left to answer the phone. Ring! Ring! Our neighbor is calling to invite us to a local fundraiser beef and beer. Hot Dog! This is what I've been waiting for! I'll just grab my dancing shoes and that sexy top and boogie on down.

Upon arrival we were welcomed by a group of people composed of all ages, sexes and sizes. Before sitting down, ACDC's song "All Night Long" blared through the speakers and persuaded my feet to shuffle onto the dance floor. There in the midst of some of my best dance moves, I turned to give my husband's rump a bump and noticed him standing still with his with mouth open and his index finger pointing to his right. Seems as I was innocently shimmying and shaking my stuff, one of the dancing queens in front of the bandstand decided to flash her boobs at the DJ and then turned in a 360-degree circle flapping her top at every red-blooded male in sight. What is going on here? Are we having Mardi Gras in January, are we on Jerry Springer, or what?

When the music changed, I grabbed my husband, who was still mesmerized by the scenery, headed for our table and sat down in a huff. My attention was drawn to the action on my left where a younger version of flashing Suzie was doing the bump and grind. She wasn't dancing like I was (can't burn too many calories that way) but was gyrating in place with one guy to her front and one to her back. At the table to my right, another girl was doing a suggestive move to a completely empty chair (guess her escort went to get a beer), and yet another one was rubbing herself all over her boyfriend.

Totally appalled by this public display of R-rated behavior, I was about to suggest we head for home when a rousing rendition of "Run Around Sue" burst forth from the speakers encouraging the entire table of mature ladies behind me to jump up and join in the chaotic frenzy. As they returned to their seats, they all, totally unsolicited, of course, detoured towards my table to give my husband high fives. This action was repeated when any of them went to the bathroom, retrieved a beer, or finished a dance.

As I sat there wondering if this was how The Fall of the Roman Empire began, the girl from the next table, who minutes before was rubbing herself all over her man, swished her hips into the chair next to, you guessed it, my unassuming mate. She sat down, rubbed his cheek, gave him a big wet kiss, and innocently asked, "Do you like my breasts?" As he explained later, not wanting to hurt her feelings, he had to reply, "Why yes I do. They look wonderful." After social niceties were exchanged, I do not know what the question was, but my spouse's answer was to point across the table and introduce me as his wife. Was that tart embarrassed? Of course not! She just laughed and hugged my significant other before she sashayed back to her own man at her own table.

Later as I heard my husband comment for the umpteenth time that this was the best night of his entire life, I remembered Flashing Suzie, Gyrating Betty, the high-five girls, and the proposition. Suspiciously, I looked at him and asked, "I was wondering if you remember watching that DVD I gave you?" To this, he replied, "OH YEAH!!"

"By the way what exactly did you wish for?" At that, he winked and calmly stated, "I can't tell you because it's a SECRET."

PART FIVE:

The Fitting End

24

The Good Old Days

"I have had enough! This is the final straw!" Yelling and sobbing uncontrollably, I threw my TV remote against the wall and watched it shatter into pieces. What caused this seemingly sane, slightly middle-aged woman to exhibit such unusual behavior, you ask? Was it that animal commercial displaying teary, furry faced dogs enclosed in cages with the accompaniment of "Amazing Grace" playing? Was it the end of Jimmy Stewart's *It's a Wonderful Life*, where the angel got her wings? What was it?!

I am sitting here weeping because after 25 minutes of watching emotional testimony of proclamations of fidelity and denials of betrayals concerning a heartbreaking situation, the DNA results are in. "Frankinjustania, you are not, I repeat *not* the father." This announcement vibrates as the camera scans faces of four anxious men who had hopes of siring an adorable baby boy. Staring at the blank wall, thoughts of what led to these frantic actions raced through my mind. Can it be jealousy that this child's mother has had more action in one month then I have experienced in years (I need to contact her social director), or the fact that with over 100 stations available, this dribble is the only thing to grab my attention? Understood, the white-haired guy of Diners, Drive-Ins, and Dives on TV holds some appeal. Just watching him feed his face with foods made with goat cheese melted in real cream will make most Americans hold their stomachs and run to the bathroom for release.

Remember when television was an anomaly that provided America with quality inspirational shows like Jack La Laine and his juicer and Debbie Drake and her exercises (pioneers born decades too early), Romper Room and The Tonight Show? Yeah, those were the days! Americans looked forward to coming home, watching a quality program that kept them awake until the witching hour of 1am, when the Star-Spangled Banner ended all TV activities until 7am the next day.

Realizing that there is no hope to bring back those good old days, I decided to concentrate on the situation at hand. I need a social life and I need one *now* (preferably with a MAN)! What to do, what to do? Where does a mature, reasonable golden girl go to find some action around these parts? Supermarket, bar scene, movie theatre, library – where?

A commercial advertisement finding love online came to mind. Hallelujah – that's the ticket! I will just join one of those online dating sites and let fate run its course. Surely, there are many fine older gentlemen searching for a spirited lass like myself. Let's see, let's see. I'll just post a somewhat sexy picture, write a snazzy profile, sit back, and let the romantic adventures begin.

Upon paying my fee, my eye was drawn to a line of red flags streaming across the screen flashing danger. DANGER - *Click Here* for advice about scam artists using this site. Pshaw! My dating techniques may be a tad rusty in this world of modern romance, but since love is love, and that has not changed in the past 50 years, I decided to muddle through and clicked *Delete* to ignore all those warnings.

Things were moving ahead splendidly as messages from several cosmopolitan men from Ireland, Germany, England and Australia were received. Yippee! this was more action than I ever got in high school and I was absolutely charmed. Excited when they all requested my email and cell phone info, a swift response was issued as time is a'wasting and, at my age, I was in no position to play hard to get.

The texts and the emails were flying back and forth at a frenzied pace, with whimsical quips being exchanged at my end but not too much information was coming from The MEN.

Two weeks later, a voice roused me from a deep sleep. *Something is not quite right here. Something is not quite right here.* Yes, something was absolutely not quite right, and it had to do with my new-found love life. It seems all my perspective suitors had the same story. They lived at least two hours away in affluent neighborhoods, came to this country in the last five to 10 years, had jobs that involved a lot of travel, were self-employed (more than one was an architect), and, mysteriously, no one wanted to meet in person. When I returned to check their profiles and pictures, all their information had conveniently disappeared from the site. Who were these men I been corresponding with for the last two weeks? Men, women, or God forbid, companies?

Maybe I am not as knowledgeable as I thought and was a bit too hasty in deleting those red flag warnings. No worries, I will just return to the surplus of available matches and take my pick. Unfortunately, when all the crooks were removed, only a bunch of frowny faced old men remained. Come on guys, you need to look more appealing and at least smile for the camera.

Just as I was about to give up on this modern method of dating and admit defeat, a message from Vern the Vitamin Man appeared. He liked that I was healthy and took supplements and wanted to meet me at a local eatery. Hot Damn! This is what I have been waiting for, real contact with a real person. His profile was not very exciting, and all 10 pictures displayed him with the same woman. But beggars can't be choosers, and I am looking at a real date with a real person.

About to reap the benefit of my online dating efforts, I splashed myself with perfume, put a smile on my face, and rushed out the door to begin a new adventure. We met at a respectable restaurant where the hostess greeted us warmly and escorted us to an intimate corner table. So far so good! The thrill of romance was in the air.

Upon being seated, he insisted on ordering not only lunch, but an appetizer and a glass of wine as well. Yeah, this is what I'm talking about, a bona fide date! Then after my first sip of wine, he began to talk about the 60 minerals you need to ingest every day to stay healthy. He went on to mention his regular bowel movements, his thick hair, and so on and so on. Alrighty then! The conversation continued as he listed each mineral separately, and what part of the body each one helped. He went on to say that if his dearly departed wife had only listened to him and taken these supplements 10 years ago, she would be here today instead of dying prematurely.

Hmmm, this calls for another sip of wine (or maybe a bottle is in order), and when is that appetizer coming? Halfway through the meal, we had covered how great and youthful his wife was (she was still being carded at the age of 45), how they met, where they went on their first date, and where they lived over the 30 years of their marriage. Could this date get any worse?

I politely asked if he had any pictures of her as I was anxious to see this fantastic female specimen. Obviously, he did not appreciate my humor because he answered, "I was going to bring a bunch displaying her beauty, but I forgot." Realizing that I had not shared one aspect of my life, since nobody was really interested, I politely thanked him for the date and, with the box of Swiss chocolates he brought in hand, headed for the exit. Ever the polite gentleman, he insisted on walking me to my car where we parted ways after agreeing that we were not a good match.

Ronnie Mundis

I heard there is a group of seniors called the Delaware Single Boomers in town. I might need to check them out.

25

Boomers Christmas Dinner

Merry Christmas, Merry Christmas! Ho! Ho! Ho! This holiday is going to be exciting because I am going to eat my Christmas dinner at a sushi restaurant with a group I recently joined called the Boomers (people born between the year 1945-1960). Hooray!! What could go wrong? I'll just put on my sparkling Gramma necklace, tight leggings, Christmas sweater, and venture out for a different social experience.

    Visions of meeting new people, having a few laughs, and enjoying myself danced in my head until I arrived and learned I had something to dread.

    Upon entering the restaurant, I was led to a table of eight somber souls, who appeared not as enthusiastic as I was to be there. The two empty seats to my left were quickly filled with a pleasant gentleman and his miserable significant other. After noticing the woman seated to my right was glaring at the man to my left, I sensed there just might be a history between those two and tried to change that negative energy by cheerfully introducing myself. My *hello-I-am-a-new-member* drew the following comment, "Oh I have seen you before and I know exactly who you are." This comment was voiced along with a scowling look from the charming lady to my right. That's strange, because I did not know any of these people and I was beginning to think I did not want to know them.

As the meal progressed, I realized that a conversation was going on through me, not with me, as people continued to talk over me. Hello, do I offend or what? Buck up old gal, this is not the worst company you have been in (always remember that Vitamin Man). I can make this work, or so I thought, until the conversation at the table continued. It included information about what company each one had retired from, where they went to grad school, how many foreign countries they have visited, their numerous accomplishments, the occupations of their children, how many ex-spouses each had, what their exes did for a living, and the vast amount of money they made.

Amid this incessant bragging, several babies at the next table began to scream. Guess the negative vibes got to even the weakest among us. Just as I was beginning to think I should have stayed home, eaten my Christmas Eve leftovers and watched the Hallmark Channel Marathon, the lady next to me started to argue with the man on my other side concerning the closing of a restaurant in a local shopping center. He was explaining how he did all the plumbing, painting, and maintenance work for 10 years on it, only to have the owner show up one day, declare he was moving to Florida, and closing the place for good.

As the conversation went on, voices were raised and ugly comments followed. Ok, so maybe he was a little annoying as he described in detail his many talents, however, the restaurant closing situation did not warrant a confrontation of this level. His significant other, less than excited about the ensuing quarrel, just kept eating and ignored everything and everyone (my kind of gal).

As he droned on about how his second wife (not the person beside him) was from Mexico and lived with him until the police showed up, handcuffed her and led her away, my ears perked up in anticipation of a colorful story that would make this experience more interesting. Little Miss Argumentative squashed that by saying, "Well that sounds like a long story, and way too long for Christmas Dinner." Wait a minute! I wanted to hear that long story as it may lift my spirits.

Before I knew it, the conversation switched from the restaurant closing to tax returns as Miss Unfriendly seated to my right proceeded to quiz the disagreeable woman to my left who apparently was a tax expert. Again, they were talking over me or looking right through me. As that conversation got aggressive and before the SWAT team was summoned to control this unruly bunch, I grabbed my check and raced out the door to my quiet home.

26

Online Dating

Do not, absolutely do *not* join that new senior online dating site you just discovered. Never mind how exciting their advertising makes it look or how many handsome men they say have left messages for you. Do not click that *Buy Now* button. As soon as you do, you will regret it as all the men and messages will disappear and leave you with a three-month automatic renewal charge that will require you to cancel your credit card to stop it.

I am realistic and know there is nothing magical about this site, however, nothing ventured nothing gained. So against my better judgment, I pressed that button and signed up for another three months of disappointments. This time will be different. I just know it.

Once I clicked on my smart picks and saw the men were at least 60 to 85 years old, I was more comfortable. Comfortable, that is, until I began to read the stories underneath several of their profiles. These men were **REMARKABLE!** Even though they were 60 and above (the time when many of us are slowing down), they had not missed a beat and maintained an exercise regimen only matched by Seal Team Six. They jog, they swim, they surf, they ski, work out every day, fish, hunt and travel to Africa, India, China and Japan. Every one of them has the stamina of a 40-year-old (if you know what I mean – Hubba, Hubba)!

Some even have x-ray vision and leap tall buildings in a single bound!! What Fountain of Youth are they drinking from? These slim, fit, energetic gents are, of course, looking for slender, trim, athletic females with long hair, who are gourmet chefs while being soft and cuddly and yet have the stamina to dance all night. The ability to clean those fish and gut that deer while wearing aprons and high heels to emphasize their feminine persona is also required.

Since, so far on other sites, I only attracted a 70-year-old man who insisted he was serving a tour of duty in Afghanistan (must have been a Brigadier General), I decided to take action and make some minor adjustments to my profile.

Let me see, I will delete the phrases: "embracing my age," "realistic about physical limitations," "gluten and lactose intolerant," and "likes to travel by bus or train." Of course, I must delete any mention of my need for those essential daily naps. I will also rephrase, "takes arthritis and cardio swim classes at the local senior center" to "swims ten laps a day in an Olympic size pool." And "walks a mile twice a week" can be changed to "speed walks five miles daily." If that doesn't get me some action, I will add "loves to cast that line and shoot that gun" (I am a regular Sarah Palin), "loves camping" (if camping means staying in a four-star hotel with room service and views of beautiful sunsets), "can dance all night long" (provided I can wear my Depends), and of course, "I love to **Hubba, Hubba.**"

In order to fit in with these big boys, I will need to step up my game and make a few adjustments to my beauty routine. First - take a hot Epson salts bath (need to limber all those old muscles and joints). Second - I'll need a manicure, pedicure, spritz of cologne, and a bit of makeup (to enhance my feminine charms). Third - I must squeeze into that Spanx (enough said). Fourth - I'll put in hair extensions to obtain the required waist-length mane. Fifth - I'll wear a sexy, yet classy, outfit which is age appropriate. And last, but not least, hang up that cane, dig out those stilettoes from the back of my closet, and get ready to boogie all night long.

Armed with the above beauty enhancements, I am ready to step out of my comfort zone and take on the world. Nothing can stop me now. Nothing, that is, unless I topple from my lofty four-inch high heels while dancing, take that deep breath to cause my Spanx to split as I lose my battle of the bulge, drop that hair extension when I bust a move, and, God forbid, fall asleep before 10:00pm.

27

STOP

"S Mississippi, T Mississippi, O Mississippi, P Mississippi, my ass."

"What did you say?" I asked. Those words were so out of character coming from my mild-mannered friend.

"I said, *my ass*," she replied.

"No, the words before that, you know the Mississippi stuff."

She walked in circles waving her hands as she started her rant. "I said, 'Stop Mississippi' because that's what one of Pennsylvania's finest made me repeat as I was given instructions on how to stop at a stop sign. I mean, it was embarrassing. With lights glaring and sirens blaring he pulled me over after I turned onto an abandoned country road. I nervously explained I had been driving for over 40 years and I certainly know the proper way to stop at a stop sign. He countered that in his book I did not stop long enough, wrote out a ticket for a $100 fine, and advised that I could go to court to appeal it if I did not agree with his judgment. I am so angry I could just spit."

With a calming voice, I suggested she just pay the fine and be happy she did not get any points on her license. Then I also reasoned going to court will just add another $50 court cost, since it is your word against his, and he is, after all, the long arm of the law. We continued to talk about more pleasant topics before the conversation ended and we went our separate ways.

Content that this upsetting situation was resolved, I left satisfied. Satisfied, that is, until the end of the next month when glaring lights and blaring sirens disrupted my peaceful drive as I was pulled over by one of Delaware's finest. Knowing that I had not gotten a ticket in 20 years, and I am ever the most careful of drivers, I pulled to the side of the road, so the officer could pass by on his way to apprehend real criminals for committing real crimes.

After 10 minutes of looking in my rearview mirror, realizing the lights were still glaring and he was just not going away, I planned my course of action. Let's see, it has been 20 years since my last traffic offense, so I may be a little rusty at this, but I think a flirty smile and a few winks might do the trick.

As the officer approached looking at least 40 years my junior, my agenda changed, as that ship sailed long ago. So now there was no recourse but to sit up straight and face the music. Assured that my spotless driving record would warrant a mere warning, I confidently handed my insurance and registration documents through the window and waited to be told I was free to go. Instead of a friendly, "Y'all drive safe now, you hear," I was presented with not only a $100 ticket, but also three points on my driver's license. (This cop wanted to get his quota in the worse way.)

It seems that besides rolling through a stop sign, I had committed the horrendous crime of having a frame around my license plate. I questioned the validity of that declaration. "A frame around a license plate that does not cover any vital information and is there solely to hold the plate in place is now a law. Are you sure that is really a law?"

"Well ma'am, two years ago, it was one of the few accomplishments of our State legislators and widely published in both State newspapers. Sorry you missed it," he sarcastically replied.

"The $100 fine is bad enough, but three points on a senior citizen's license is a disaster. Can't you give a golden girl a break?"

To that he smirked while pointing to the ticket. "Just call that number and you may get some of those points lifted."

As I watched him saunter to his shiny cruiser, my anger rose with feelings of being violated. My personal space had been invaded for no good reason, and I was mad! So mad I could just spit!! But instead, I drove all the way home shouting words never to be found in the *How to be The Best Gramma in the World* book."

Upon arriving at my domain, several solutions to this problem came to mind. I could either just ignore the ticket and do nothing (result: possible jail time when I go to renew my license), or pay the $100 fine and accept the three points (result: losing my license after my next stop sign roll). Then there is the third option, which is to put on my big girl panties and call the number to schedule a court date (result: lots of stress and aggravation, but possible reduction of those pesky points).

After fortifying myself with a few glasses of wine, I accepted option three as my only course of action. I picked up the phone and dialed. As I began to issue my request, a machine interrupted with the following: "Hello and welcome to traffic court. To request a hearing, please send a letter explaining why you think your situation justifies our consideration to the following address. If deemed acceptable you will then receive a reply informing you of our decision."

Who replaced the old method of simply checking a box on a citation and mailing it in with this lengthy procedure? Could it possibly be the legislators who passed that all-important license plate frame law? If it is a letter they want, a letter they will get. It will be filled with an assortment of repentant words to tug the heartstrings of the grumpiest among them. I may even receive a full pardon and not have to appear in court at all.

Two weeks later, a notice came in the mail stating that my letter had been received, reviewed, deemed acceptable, and a court date had been granted. It became apparent my efforts had been in vain. I was headed for my first traffic court appearance.

On the day of judgment, having nightmares of being detained and led to the Big House, the Slammer, the Lockup, the Pen, I was surprised to see that traffic court was just another office located in a regular looking building. Suspicious, as there were at least 30 people in line ahead of me, my eyes focused on the sign above which read: "Traffic court is open 7 days a week, 24 hours a day." Then the purpose of my citations became clear. This was not about making me a better driver at all but merely another money-making machine.

It's Funny Because It's True

Casting the evidence to fight these charges aside, my new plan was to play on the judge's sympathies for the elderly and beg for mercy. Upon taking a seat, I noticed other traffic violators were shuffling through the door, wearing oversized, face-covering hoodies and carrying crying babies. I was not feeling the warm and fuzzy here, and was relieved when my name was called directing me to enter the first door to my right.

Small room, pleasant looking officer with a big smile on his face – this I can handle. He read my letter, looked at me, heard my plea for mercy as to my ignorance of the license plate frame law, checked to see who issued the violation, exclaimed "Oh my God!" and threw out that charge. Alrighty then, this was easier than I thought. Unfortunately, he was only the traffic counselor and I still had to appear in front of the official judge for my stop sign roll violation. It was back to my seat in the waiting area surrounded by all those hooded, faceless people.

Then 10 minutes later, after entering a larger room with yet another pleasant looking chap, I hung my head and remorsefully explained that I thought I had stopped long enough, but the arresting officer did not see it my way, and I was ever so sorry (sniffle, sniffle, boo-hoo). My hopes rose as the Judge read my letter, examined my 20-year spotless driving record, shook his head in dismay and commented, "Oh my God, who pulled you over for this?" Then reading further, he said, "Figures it was Sullivan." He was very apologetic as he explained my two options. I could stay for a trial and face the arresting officer or pay the $100 fine plus court costs and be on my way. Instead of the two-year no further violation rule for the points to be reported to my insurance company, he was going to lower my time to one year. Excited at my good fortune, I took the lesser option, paid my fine and ran out the door.

Two months later when the local senior center advertised that they were offering a defensive driving course which would lower your car insurance premiums, I decided to take it as a hedge against any future mishaps. Looking at the first sentence of the first paragraph in the driving manual, an uncontrollable laugh escaped when I saw "S Mississippi, T Mississippi, O Mississippi, P Mississippi."

28

Boot Scooting

Boot Scooting, Boot Scooting. That is what my road to romance needs - a little boot scooting. After all, it helped Debra Winger and John Travolta fall in love in *Urban Cowboy* and, gosh darn, it was going to help me! Now all I need to do is learn that dance, buy snazzy cowgirl boots and that all important hat, and get ready for the romantic bliss to follow.

Luckily, the local senior center is offering a new class on learning to line dance. Even though that is not quite boot scooting, it is movement to country music. So, lead me to that signup sheet and let the fun begin!

The day of the first class finally arrived and I, along with five other healthy-looking senior ladies, entered the gym ready for a new adventure. Recognizing four of them from my arthritis swimming class (one a 90-year-old), I felt assured that keeping up with this group would be no problem. My confidence soared when a newcomer stated, "I hope this is not too strenuous as I am recuperating from knee surgery." Then a little voice in my head whispered, *Go on, stand next to her. She will make you look good.* That is how I ended up in the front row, ready to boot scoot, when our instructor arrived.

He was a handsome looking gentleman who cheerfully presented us with a brochure that contained numerous homework assignments. Homework, this class has *homework*? Just a minute now, I believe I signed up for fun not homework. The assignments included such things as smile, talk, and have fun meeting new people, along with the names and steps of several line dances, so I decided to stay and enjoy the experience.

We started off slow enough with a dance called the Continental. Step together step, step back, stomp, stomp were the vocal instructions shouted out while we all sang along while carefully moving our feet to the music. This is a piece of cake. Don't know what I was worried about. Slow and easy you go. As we looked around smiling at each other, another step was added and the tempo increased to double time. A little challenging but nothing that cannot be handled by this over 64-year-old group. About 10 minutes into that routine, people began dropping like flies. I heard: "Stop the music." "I am going to have a heart attack." "I need to sit down." "I need a bathroom break."

The host graciously agreed and gave us 10 minutes to catch our breath, get a drink of water, refresh and regroup. Now there were only four of us left on the dance floor, as the other two decided to sit and observe. Another dance was introduced with more movement at a faster pace. Hearing the comment, "Hey you are really good at this," I threw myself into the rhythm of the beat and was just dancing away. Dancing that is, until a glance at the knee surgery lady showed me what all the excitement was about. She was doing Charleston moves that would shame a 1920's flapper. Where did those moves come from? For Pete's sakes what about your rebuilt knee? Not to be undone, I threw myself into the next jazz turn, felt my knee buckle, and saw myself rapidly approaching the floor. With visions of the paramedics being called to hoist me up and take me to the emergency room, I mustered a burst of energy, caught myself in mid-fall, and awkwardly stumbled towards the nearest chair.

A glance at the wall clock informed me this half-hour class was over. (Thank You, Jesus!) As I began to gather my things and head for home, my 90-year-old swimming buddy exclaimed, "Where are you going? This is an hour class and there are 15 minutes left." Knowing I would never last through 15 more minutes of this torture, I pulled myself off that chair, shoulders back, chest-high and with a wobbly gait, limped towards the exit.

The next week in swimming class when asked how the line dancing class was going, my fellow dance classmate put her arm around me and announced to everyone, "Didn't you hear? She is a line dancing school dropout." Now I know

It's Funny Because It's True

how Frenchy, the Beauty School Dropout from the movie *Grease*, felt.

29

And on We Go!

As I travel through this adventure called life, I have learned that nothing is definite. A well-planned trip to the doctor, the store, a concert, or a dance can quickly depart from the scheduled agenda. Even a day at work can take an unexpected twist or turn at any moment. Encounters with people we meet along the way often make everyday situations unpredictable and quite interesting. I have written this book to share events in my life that I find quite humorous. It is my hope that others can relate to some of these stories, enjoy reading them, and laugh along with me. Life is a journey - so on we go! I can't wait to write about what happens next.

Acknowledgments

I would like to acknowledge the colorful characters who came into my life and provided the material to make me laugh.

About the Author

Ronnie Mundis is pretty much a jack of all trades. Her jobs working as a schoolteacher, waitress, band manager, daycare owner, credit card representative, and property manager have given her a trove of material for writing about people and life. Ronnie lives in Wilmington, Delaware where she continues to write about things that are just too funny.

Made in the USA
Middletown, DE
10 November 2019